Unmasking Mormonism

Who are the Latter-day Saints?

Selwyn Stevens

PUBLISHED BY

 Additional copies of this book are available from many bookstores, libraries, or from:

Jubilee Resources, PO Box 36-044, Wellington 6330, New Zealand,
Jubilee Resources, PO Box 1412, Sunnybank Hills, Qld 4109, Australia,
Jubilee Resources, PO Box 4174, Evansville IN 47724-4174, USA,
Jubilee Resources, PO New Hamburg, Ontario N0B 2G0 Canada
or our Internet Web site bookshop at www.jubilee-resources.com

New Zealand Edition printed December 1994
Second Printing July 1996 revised & expanded
Third Printing July 2000, revised and expanded

ISBN 0-9583569-3-9

<u>Your guarantee of accurate Information:</u> various sources and authorities have been quoted in good faith throughout this book. Every attempt has been made to ensure these quotations are accurate and in context.

DEDICATION

This book is dedicated to the Saints of God who toil to bring the light of the Gospel of Jesus Christ to people ensnared in the spiritual darkness and deception of secret societies, cults and occultism. The author wishes to acknowledge and thank many people too numerous to mention here who have given advice and encouragement to put this message into print.

CONTENTS

INTRODUCTION

My priority in this series of books, "the Unmasking of Deception," is three fold.

* First, it is intended to inform and equip Christians about groups which claim to be Christian, but which can be clearly shown are not.

* Secondly, I hope to provide compelling information which would persuade a person considering joining the Latter-day Saints (Mormon) Church that they are in danger of deception. Everyone needs reliable information before making any decision about getting involved with any group, whether it is a controversial cult or not.

* Thirdly, it is my prayer that those entangled in cults like the Mormon. Church will recognise there is a salvation-threatening difference between what they are being taught in their church, and what God teaches us in His trustworthy Word, the Bible.

If something is true it can stand being questioned. But if it is not true, then it needs to be questioned. I do not seek to attack or belittle individual Mormons in this book. If you are a Mormon, or thinking of joining them, you have the right to check out the claims made by the Mormon Church and also those who expose it, to seek the truth. I invite you is to check the references provided to confirm that what I have written here is both true and contextual. This book is a search for the truth and also a calling for integrity in the face of deception. It will not be popular with LDS leaders because it exposes many facts which have been deliberately kept from their members. This evidence will show that Mormons are deceived by their own leaders into a false and ineffective salvation, one which is no salvation at all. Don't assume that good morals make a good religion, for God Himself says that isn't enough.

In the last decade, the Mormon Church has dispatched over 220,000 missionaries for terms of about two years to knock on doors in neighbourhoods like yours and mine. Worldwide the fruit of their labours has resulted in almost 50,000 converts every month. In New Zealand the Mormon Church is presently the fifth largest religious organisation, and has recently swapped positions with the Baptist denomination.

Christians have a job to do with all speed; to know the God of the Bible and His Word much better, so they can share with others the love and certain hope of Eternal Life that they have in Jesus Christ. I also hope the Christian Church will not see cults as a threat but as a potential mission field. My prayer is that this book series may assist in some small way to achieve that purpose, and I entrust it all to the Living God for His divine purposes to be fulfilled.

THE CHALLENGE AND THE INVITATION

Brigham Young

It was Brigham Young, second president of the Mormon Church, who challenged the world to ***"Take up your Bible, compare the religion of the Latter-day Saints with it, and see if it stand the test."***[1]

To confirm this offer, it was repeated in these words by Joseph Fielding Smith, the LDS Tenth Prophet. He said ***"Mormonism must stand or fall on the story of Joseph Smith. He was either a prophet of God... or one of the biggest frauds this world has ever seen. If his claims and declarations were built upon fraud and deceit there would appear many errors and contradictions which would be easy to detect... If Joseph Smith was a deceiver, who wilfully attempted to mislead people, then he should be exposed; his claims should be refuted, and his doctrines shown to be false, for the doctrines of an imposter cannot be made to harmonise in all particulars with divine truth."***[2]

MORMON SCRIPTURES AND THEIR CONTRADICTIONS

Joseph F. Smith

To check out these offers we need to understand that Mormons accept three other books as being of equal or greater authority than the Bible. These are "The Book of Mormon," "Doctrines & Covenants" and the "Pearl of Great Price." In their Articles of Faith they do claim the Bible (and only the King James Version of it) is the Word of God, ***"...as far as it is translated correctly."*** The Mormon leaders have had over 160 years to provide any compelling evidence or documentation to prove their claims of incorrect translation, and have failed to do so. The cynic might say that this is a convenient way of avoiding the many anti-Biblical errors and heresies contained in much Mormon writing. We will investigate these later.

There are other authoritative books such as Bruce R. McConkie's "Mormon Doctrine," "Journals & Discourses," etc. Only some of these books are accepted by the other 215 Mormon breakaway groups or denominations. I am writing about the largest group which is based in Salt Lake City, Utah. (By the way, the Mormons take no offence at their nickname but prefer their correct title of "The Church of Jesus Christ of Latter-day Saints.") On many key doctrines these so-called scriptures contradict each other, as we see in the charts on the following two pages.

TOPIC	MORMON SCRIPTURE SAYS	CONTRASTING MORMON SCRIPTURE SAYS	THE BIBLE (NEW KING JAMES VERSION)
IS GOD AN EXALTED MAN?	NO! "Believest thou that this Great Spirit, who is God, created all things," (Alma 18:28, BOM).	YES! "The Father has a body of flesh and bones as tangible as man's, the Son also..." (D&C,130:22)	NO! "God is Spirit," (John 4:24); "God is not a man...nor a son of man," (Numbers 23:19).
FATHER, SON & THE HOLY SPIRIT ARE THE ONE GOD	YES! "Which Father, Son and Holy Ghost are one God, infinite and eternal," (D&C 20:28).	NO! "Father, Son and Holy Ghost comprise the Godhead. As each of these persons is a God...a plurality of Gods exists," (MD, pps 576-7)	YES! "For there are these three who bear witness in heaven: the Father, the Word, and the Holy Spirit; and these three are one," (1 John 5:7).
GOD IS ETERNAL	YES! "For I know that God is not a partial God, neither a changeable being; but he is unchangeable from all eternity to all eternity," (Moroni 8:18 BOM).	NO! "We have imagined and supposed that God was God from all eternity. I will refute that idea," (MD, p 321).	YES! "The eternal God is your refuge," (Deut. 33:27).
GOD CHANGES	NO! "There is a God in heaven, who is infinite and eternal, from everlasting to everlasting, the same unchangeable God," (D&C 20:17).	YES! "We believe in a God who is Himself progressive... whose perfection consists in eternal advancement..." (Articles of Faith, p 430).	NO! "For I am the LORD, I do not change," (Malachi 3:6).
THERE IS A PLURALITY OF GODS.	NO! "The Father and the Son and the Holy Ghost are one... and whoso shall declare more or less than this, and establish it for my doctrine, the same cometh of evil," (3 Nephi 11:27, 4 BOM)	YES! "These three are the only Gods we worship. But in addition there is an infinite number of holy personages, drawn from worlds without number, who...are gods," (MD, p 576 - 7).	NO! "I am He. Before Me there was no God formed, nor shall there be after Me," (Isaiah 43:10).
CAN MEN BE GODS?	NO! "Now Zeezrom said: Is there more than one God? And he answered, NO,"(Alma 11:28,29 BOM).	YES! "Then shall they (those resurrected) be gods, because they have no end," (D&C 132:20).	NO! "Thus says the LORD... Besides me there is no God," (Isaiah 44:6).
GOD CREATED MAN	YES! "And I, God, created man in mine own image," (Moses 2:27, PGP).	NO! "Man was also in the beginning with God...For man is spirit," (D&C 93:29,33).	YES! " And the LORD God formed man..." (Genesis 2:7).
CAN GOD BE SEEN?	NO! "For without this (the authority of the Priesthood) no man can see the face of God, even the Father and live," (D&C 84:22). (Smith did not have Priesthood when he claimed to see God.)	YES! "And he (Moses) saw God face to face, and he talked with him... Moses could endure his presence," (Moses 1:2, PGP).	NO! "No man has seen God at any time... The only begotten Son ...has declared Him," (John 1:18).

TOPIC	MORMON SCRIPTURE SAYS	CONTRASTING MORMON SCRIPTURE SAYS	THE BIBLE (NEW KING JAMES VERSION)
JESUS IS THE ONE TRUE GOD	YES! "Blessed be the name of the Most High God. And they did fall down at the feet of Jesus and did worship him," (3 Nephi 11:17 BOM).	NO! "Jesus Christ is a separate and distinct personage...three distinct personages and three gods," (Teachings of the Prophet Joseph Smith, by J.F. Smith, p 370).	YES! "Now to the King eternal, immortal, invisible, to God who alone is wise..." (Speaking of Jesus Christ)(1 Timothy,1:17)
JESUS CHRIST IS ETERNAL	YES! "...from all eternity to all eternity, the Great I AM, even Jesus Christ," (D&C 39:1).	NO! "Christ, the Firstborn, was the mightiest of all the spirit children of the Father," (MD, p 590).	YES! "...whose goings forth have been from of old, From everlasting," (Micah 5:2).
JESUS WAS BORN OF A VIRGIN	YES! "And behold, he shall be born of Mary at Jerusalem, she being a virgin,"(Alma7:10 BOM).	NO! "Christ was begotten by the Immortal Father in the same way that mortal men are begotten by mortal fathers," (MD, p 547).	YES! "After His mother Mary was betrothed to Joseph, before they came together, she was found with child of the Holy Spirit," (Matthew 1:18)
THE WAY TO SALVATION IS JESUS	YES! "Behold, Jesus Christ is the name... there is none other name whereby man can be saved," (D&C 18:23).	NO! "The President of the Church of Jesus Christ of Latter Day Saints holds the keys of salvation for all men now living..." (MD, p 411).	YES! "For there is one God and one mediator between God and men, the Man Christ Jesus," (1 Timothy 2:5).
CHRIST'S BLOOD CLEANSES US FROM ALL SIN	YES! "...salvation was, and is, and is to come, in and through the atoning blood of Christ, the Lord Omnipotent," (Mosiah 3:18 BOM).	NO! "...for the blood of Christ alone under certain circumstances will not avail," (for atonement of sin) (MD, p 93).	YES! "...and the blood of Jesus Christ His Son cleanses us from all sin," (1 John 1:7).
IS THERE SALVATION AFTER DEATH?	NO! "For behold, if ye have procrastinated the day of your repentance even until death... the devil hath all power over you; and this is the final state of the wicked," (Alma 34:35 BOM).	YES! "...in relation to the dead...For their salvation is necessary and essential to our salvation...that they without us cannot be made perfect," (D&C, 128:15).	NO! "And as it is appointed for men to die once, but after this the judgement," (Hebrews 9:27).
HELL IS EVERLASTING DESTRUCTION	YES! "Yes, they were encircled about by the bands of death, and the chains of hell, and an everlasting destruction did await them," (Alma 5:7 BOM).	NO!"Whosoever, therefore receives God's punishment receives eternal punishment, whether it is endured one hour, one day, one week, one year, or an age," (Plan of Salvation, page 30, pamphlet distributed by Elders).	YES! "And the smoke of their torment ascends forever and ever, and they have no rest day or night..." (Revelation 14:11).

(Abbreviations used: BOM = Book of Mormon, D&C = Doctrine & Covenants, PGP = Pearl of Great Price, MD = Mormon Doctrine by Bruce R.McConkie.)

Clearly Mormon authorities do contradict each other! They will regard our investigation into their beliefs, practices and history here as persecution.[3a] But may I ask what is it when Mormons tell me that the Christian Church is an abomination; that professing Christians are corrupt; that our pastors are weak hirelings of the devil and that the Bible is untrustworthy?[3] Is that persecution or just plain abusive? Let us now take up the second challenge of their Tenth Prophet and look at the founder of this new religious organisation.

JOSEPH SMITH JUNIOR

Joseph Smith is crucial to Mormonism. In fact Brigham Young, their second President, insists that everyone's salvation depends on Smith, and even claims it is Joseph who will issue the certificates for entry into God's presence for judgement and exaltation to the celestial kingdom.[4] It is also claimed that Joseph and Adam helped Jesus create the Earth. That conflicts with the Genesis account, as well as Colossians 1:16, where it records that Jesus created all things, including Adam and Joseph.[5] So, who is this man who pretends to judge all others? Is he worthy of such an elevated position?

Joseph Smith Jnr.

The fourth child of Joseph and Lucy Smith, he was largely uneducated, undisciplined and illiterate.[6] It is claimed that in 1820, when in his mid-teens, Joseph Smith had what is called his "First Vision." This had such a profound effect on young Joseph that he then ignored it for at least three years. He didn't even write down what he saw for several years. Over the following two decades he wrote at least six differing versions of this vision. These don't agree on how old Smith was at the time; whether Smith saw one, two or several "godly personages" (the 1835 version fails to mention God or Christ at all, but says only many spirits or "angels"); what Smith's purpose was at the time; and quite a number of other important facts. One version states the personage was the angel Nephi, while another version says it was the angel Moroni. Smith claimed there had been a religious revival occurring at that time (1820), causing him to seek God. There are at least three separate historic records which show the revival mentioned didn't begin until September 1824 and lasted about twelve months. These are all significant discrepancies which tend to question Smith's credibility.

His father, who had the same name, was widely known as a mystic who had visions, dreams and trances, and who used divination while attempting to locate hidden treasure. He also "sold blessings." He even got into trouble with the law while counterfeiting coins. Young Joseph's mother, Lucy Mack Smith, was a known clairvoyant and fortune teller, deeply involved in the occult. Nowadays this couple would probably attend a Spiritualist church. There is overwhelming evidence that young Joe grew up in a family and social environment where spiritualism was widely practised. Joseph Junior was widely known (like his father) for using various forms of divination, including dowsing rods or sticks, and "peek stones," to locate lost objects, fortune-telling, and to seek buried treasure. Apparently he used a common witchcraft practice of sacrificing an animal, and sprinkling the blood to break the spell guarding the supposed "buried treasure." This finally got Joe into trouble when he took money from people but failed to deliver any treasure. The State of New York took Joe to court, and he was convicted on March 20 1826, in Bainbridge by Justice Albert Neely. There is no such thing as Christian divination or spiritualism, just as there can't be Christian adultery or Christian murder. The term "Christian Spiritualism" is a contradiction in terms, and God records plainly in the Bible His condemnation of all involved in the spiritualist practices used by the Smiths and others.

Neighbours such as Judge Daniel Woodard and Rev. Dr. John Clark were not shy in exposing the Smith family. Sixty-two of the Smith's neighbours in Palmyra, New York, signed a petition against them, describing both father and son as entirely destitute of moral character, and calling Joe Junior ***"untruthful, addicted to vicious habits and a philanderer,"***[7] (an old-fashioned word for a promiscuous person).

One revealing document comes from Joseph Lewis, (a Methodist and also a cousin to Emma Smith, Joseph Smith's wife). Lewis, along with lay preacher Joshua McKane, on hearing of Joseph Smith's application to join the Methodist church in 1828, decided to challenge Smith. ***"We thought it was a disgrace to the church to have a practising necromancer, a dealer in enchantments and bleeding ghosts, in it...*** (we) ***told him*** (Smith) ***that his occupation, habits and moral character were at variance with the discipline, that his name would be a disgrace to the church, and there should have been a recantation, confession and at least promised reformation - that he*** (Smith) ***could that day publicly ask that his name be stricken from the (register of membership), or stand investigation. He chose the former."***[8] Why did Smith seek to join a Christian church in 1828, when only a few years earlier he had claimed God told him emphatically not to join one as they were all wrong?

In 1837 Joe Junior printed $3 notes under the name of "The Kirtland Safety Society anti Banking Company." However, because this money was not soundly backed by real wealth, the whole banking scheme collapsed almost immediately. The sample shown includes the signatures of both Joseph Smith Junior and Sidney Rigdon, who had been Smith's First Counsellor of the LDS church for four years.

Sidney Rigdon

There is some evidence that Sidney may have been the perpetrator of the Gold Plates hoax we shall look at shortly.[9] As the result of their bogus bank, both men had to escape from the law, and ended up in Illinois. It is known that Smith joined the Masonic Lodge in Nauvoo, Illinois, on March 15, 1842. His brother, Hyrum, had joined the Mt. Moriah Lodge several years earlier. Joseph gave himself an unauthorised promotion overnight, raising himself from the first degree to the 32nd degree. He then began teaching the masonic secrets to his church leadership on May 2, 1842, calling them "divine revelations."[10] (Please see page 37.) This exposing of Masonic secrets resulted in over one thousand Mormons, including Smith, being expelled from the Lodge. In view of the death oaths involved in Masonry, this could be a possible cause for Smith's death.

JOSEPH THE PROPHET?

A true prophet of God will never teach or proclaim anything which is contrary to the Bible. Deuteronomy 18:20-22 outlines the test of a true prophet. So does this passage; **"If there arises among you a prophet or a dreamer of dreams, and he gives you a sign or a wonder, and the sign or wonder comes to pass, of which he spoke to you, saying 'Let us go down after other gods which you have not know, and let us serve them,' you shall not listen to the words of that prophet or dreamer of dreams, for the Lord your God is testing you to know whether you love the Lord your God with all your heart and with all your soul. But that prophet or that dreamer of dreams shall be put to death, because he has spoken in order to turn you away from the Lord your God, who brought you out of the land of Egypt and redeemed you from the house of bondages, to entice you from the way in which the Lord your God**

commanded you to walk. So you shall put away the evil from your midst." (Deut. 13:1-3,5). Let us look at a few examples of Joseph Smith's prophecies;

* Smith prophesied that his son (Joseph the Third) would succeed him, but Brigham Young took over instead, and rebaptised all the followers. (The third Joseph, along with Lucy Mack Smith, established a breakaway church in Missouri, known as "The Reorganised Church of Jesus Christ of Latter-day Saints." This still exists and has about 200,000 followers. Both still claim to be the one true church.)

* In 2 Nephi 30:6, Smith originally prophesied around 1830 that the Lamanites (North American Indians) would turn ***"white and delightsome"*** within a few generations. In 1981 this verse was altered to ***"pure and delightsome,"*** once it was clear the Indians weren't changing their skin colour after 150 years.

* In 1832 Smith stated the New Jerusalem would be built on the Temple Lot in Missouri,[53] within Smith's generation. The Temple Lot is still vacant to this day and hasn't been owned by the Utah LDS church for many decades.

* In 1835 Joseph prophesied the Lord's return in 56 years, i.e. 1891.[11] Smith went on to claim ***"The Son of Man will not come in the clouds of heaven until I am 85 years old."***[11a] Jesus didn't return in 1891, and Smith was killed in 1844, so he was wrong on both counts.

* Joseph Smith introduced polytheism, so he qualified as a false prophet according to Deuteronomy 6:4 and 1 Corinthians 8:4-6. A true prophet of God cannot bring or confirm false prophecies.

At least 64 times Joseph prophesied in God's name, and no less than 58 prophecies failed to come true, according to G.T. Harrison,[12] and many other researchers. Joseph Smith Junior's life lacks any basis to be taken seriously as a true prophet of God. In fact, his early death may possibly be the result of God's judgement as revealed in the Scripture shown above. Only God knows that for sure.

The God of the Bible was not the source of Joseph Smith's revelations. The problem is that those who followed Smith (including those who follow him today) have not measured his words and deeds against those of the Bible. If they had, they would not have been deceived into following him. A false prophecy is a lie - a sin against God. It proves that God didn't send him. Such a person speaks out of **"the deceit of his heart,"** (Jeremiah 14:14). The evidence is conclusive: Joseph Smith Junior was a false prophet.

JOSEPH THE MARTYR?

Smith is portrayed to this day by the Mormon church as a martyr who sealed his own testimony of the Book of Mormon with his own blood. The facts are quite different, and are hidden from and unknown to most Mormon members. Because Smith had a "revelation" that polygamy could be practised by Mormon leaders, there was a lot of opposition from the surrounding community as well as from many Mormons. One of Smith's former assistant presidents of the LDS church, John C. Bennett, boldly exposed the polygamy in Nauvoo, Illinois. When the local newspaper "The Nauvoo Expositor," printed the allegations, Smith ordered the paper's building burned down.[13] No freedom of the press there.

John C. Bennett

Smith's own First and Second Counsellors, Austin Cowley and William Law, told the authorities what had happened, and this resulted in Smith and his brother Hyrum being put in the Carthage jail. Two other Mormon leaders were also in the jail; John Taylor (later the third prophet) and Willard Richard, both of whom survived. More than two hundred local people were demonstrating angrily outside on June 27, 1844. Some sources suggested that the Smith brothers decided to break out and make a run for it, while others said the mob broke into the jail. Whichever way it happened, Joseph managed to kill two men and wound a third before both brothers were gunned down in typical wild west fashion.[14] The point is that martyrs don't shoot back. Joseph Smith Junior was definitely not a martyr.

Hyrum Smith

Joseph is also on record as having given the Masonic sign of distress while under fire prior to dying. One theory which is difficult to prove from this distance of time is that the Freemasons organised the mob outside the jail because Joseph had broken his sacred oath never to reveal the Masonic secrets he and Hyrum had learned while members. This would be consistent with the feelings of the time in American Freemasonry, particularly with the mystery disappearance and murder of Captain William Morgan in 1826 for exposing similar Masonic secrets. Joseph was known to have taught many Masonic secrets to the Mormon leadership only six weeks prior to his death, claiming they were divine inspiration and direction for the LDS church. (See page 37 for details of the similarities.)

"The effect of this murder was to translate Joseph Smith from a mediocrity with an extravagant imagination into a martyr in the minds of his followers," wrote author and researcher, Horton Davies.[15]

BRIGHAM YOUNG

After Smith's death, Brigham Young took over the leadership, expelling anyone who opposed him, including Sidney Rigdon. Young then led his followers on a long trek to what is now Utah. (In 1847 this was Mexican territory, but Utah was permitted to joined the United States in 1895, after the Mormon leaders received a "revelation" that polygamy was wrong and then renounced it as official Mormon doctrine. This was a condition of the American federal government, which had been threatening to expel the Mormons and confiscate their property.) Young died in 1877, leaving a fortune of over $400,000, 27 wives and 56 children. (Joseph left over 40 wives behind him - at least seven were still married to other living men at the same time. [16]) It has been admitted since 1990 by some Mormon leaders that polygamy is still practised by between 30,000 and 50,000 Mormons today in Utah, although not with the public approval of the LDS Church leaders.

THE BOOK OF MORMON

About seven years after the "First Vision" Smith claimed that an angel told him where to dig for some gold plates. With the help of two crystals set as a pair of spectacles, it was alleged Smith was able to translate the writing on these gold plates. Smith is said to have sat behind a curtain and read to his secretary, Oliver Cowdery.[17] The result was published as "The Book of Mormon" with Smith claiming it as ***"the inspired word of God,"*** and ***"the most correct of any book on earth."*** If this was so correct, why have more than 4,000 changes been made to the text since the 1830 edition?

In a nutshell let me explain that the Book of Mormon is the story about two waves of Jewish people who it is claimed travelled to North America via the Atlantic Ocean. The first group were said to come directly from the Tower of Babel, and later died out. The second group is alleged to have travelled from Jerusalem around 600 BC, and were later visited by Jesus after His resurrection. Splitting into two groups, the Lamanites and the Nephites had many battles culminating in a huge one in 385 AD at Cumorah, said to be in what is now New York State. The darker skinned Lamanites annihilated the lighter skinned Nephites. It is also claimed that up to 500,000 casualties fell at Cumorah, yet not a single piece of archeological evidence has ever been presented to confirm this battle. That is very unusual as battles of this magnitude usually leave plenty of signs such as bones, weapons and armour etc.

Careful research has shown that parts of the Book of Mormon can be termed inspired; there are 27,000 words copied directly from the King James Bible! Quotations are word-for-word, often of considerable length and including whole chapters such as Isaiah 2,4 & 53. 400 verses have been taken straight from the New Testament. These have caused no end of embarrassment to the LDS church for many years, because these cannot be explained away.

Compare the following:

Moroni 10	&	*1 Corinthians 12:1-11*
1 Nephi 14	&	*Isaiah 4*
1 Nephi 20 -21	&	*Isaiah 48 - 49*
2 Nephi 12	&	*Isaiah 2*
Mosaiah 14	&	*Isaiah 53*
3 Nephi 13:1-18	&	*Matthew 6:1-23*
3 Nephi 24 - 25	&	*Malachi 3 - 4*

Despite the addition of genuine Scripture, the Book of Mormon has some credibility problems which Mormon leadership has been unable to explain. Let us look at some of the better-known examples.

* The book claims Jesus was born in Jerusalem (Alma 7:10); while the Bible states Bethlehem (Micah 5:2 & Matthew 1:21).

* It claims a ***"furious wind"*** took 344 days to get the Jaredite barge to America, which means an average speed of less than 1 mile per hour considering the distance.

* Alma 46:15, dated at 73BC by Mormon authorities, records the naming of believers as ***"Christians."*** Acts 11:36 reveals this happened first in Antioch around 42AD. How can believers in Christ be called Christians about 70 years prior to His birth?

* If North America were uninhabited until the arrival of Nephi's ship, what explanation can be given as to why they found domesticated animals, including cattle, asses, horses, goats etc., in 1 Nephi 18:25?

* 2 Nephi 3:5-15 is claimed to be a prophecy that Joseph Smith would be a descendant of Joseph, (the son of Jacob in the Bible). But 2 Nephi 3 purports that Smith was a descendant of Lehi in America. Mormon 6:11-15 and 8:2-3 show the annihilation of all Nephites so Smith has to be a Lamanite (an Indian) or the Book of Mormon contains a false prophecy. The Smith family genealogy shows they came from England.[18]

BOOK OF MORMON

I Nephi 10

8 Yea, even he should go forth and cry in the wilderness: Prepare ye the way of the Lord, and make his paths straight; for there standeth one among you whom ye know not; and he is mightier than I, whose shoe's latchet I am not worthy to unloose. And much spake my father concerning this thing.

9 And my father said he should baptize in Bethabara, beyond Jordan; and he also said he should baptize with water; even that he should baptize the Messiah with water.

10 And after he had baptized the Messiah with water, he should behold and bear record that he had baptized the Lamb of God, who should take away the sins of the world.

I Nephi 22

20 And the Lord will surely prepare a way for his people, unto the fulfilling of the words of Moses, which he spake, saying: A prophet shall the Lord your God raise up unto you, like unto me; him shall ye hear in all things whatsoever he shall say unto you. And it shall come to pass that all those who will not hear that prophet shall be cut off from among the people.

II Nephi 9

39 O, my beloved brethren, remember the awfulness in transgressing against that Holy God, and also the awfulness of yielding to the enticings of that cunning one. Remember, to be carnally-minded is death, and to be spiritually-minded is life eternal.

KING JAMES BIBLE

Matthew 3

3 For this is he that was spoken of by the prophet Esaias, saying, The voice of one crying in the wilderness, Prepare ye the way of the Lord, make his paths straight.

Luke 3

16 John answered, saying unto *them* all, I indeed baptize you with water; but one mightier than I cometh, the latchet of whose shoes I am not worthy to unloose: he shall baptize you with the Holy Ghost and with fire:

John 1

26 John answered them, saying, I baptize with water: but there standeth one among you, whom ye know not;

27 He it is, who coming after me is preferred before me, whose shoe's latchet I am not worthy to unloose.

28 These things were done in Bethabara beyond Jordan, where John was baptizing.

John 1

29 ¶ The next day John seeth Jesus coming unto him, and saith, Behold the Lamb of God, which taketh away the sin of the world.

Acts 3

22 For Moses truly said unto the fathers, A prophet shall the Lord your God raise up unto you of your brethren, like unto me; him shall ye hear in all things whatsoever he shall say unto you.

23 And it shall come to pass, *that* every soul, which will not hear that prophet, shall be destroyed from among the people.

Romans 8

6 For to be carnally minded is death; but to be spiritually minded is life and peace.

Selected verses from the Book of Mormon compared with Bible verses which appear in the King James Version, first printed in 1611 AD. The case for plagiarism by Joseph Smith in very convincing.

* If Nephi were truly a pre-Christian prophet, as is claimed, why did he use verbatim quotes from the 17th century Westminster Confession of Faith?[19] Some researchers have found excerpts from Shakespeare and a Methodist book of discipline? Does this suggest that the Church of England, Shakespeare and the Wesleys also had access to these gold plates? I think not. It confirms that the Book of Mormon was written after these other writings and borrowed freely from them.

THE MISSING DOCTRINES

The Mormon Church claims the Book of Mormon contains the "Fullness of the Gospel." If that is so then why are many of the major doctrines of the Mormon church not found in the Book of Mormon? Let me list a few of the major ones;

* *The Law of Eternal Progression* ***(see page 26)***
* *God is married.*
* *Jesus is Lucifer's spirit brother.*
* *The "holy " principle of plural marriage.*
* *That it is wrong to question their authorities (or leaders).*
* *Revelations can be altered.*
* *Jesus was just a saved being.*
* *Some sins are so grievous you must atone for them with your own blood.*
* *Adam was the archangel Michael.*
* *The Holy Ghost and the Holy Spirit are two distinctly different deities.*
* *It is essential for your salvation that you accept Joseph Smith.*
* *Men can become gods.*
* *There are many gods.*
* *Jesus was the result of a physical relationship between the Father and Mary.*
* *Each member of the Trinity is a separate god.*
* *Eternal life means you will also have spirit offspring in eternity.*
* *Baptism for the dead.*
* *Aaronic Priesthood for non-Levites.*

Let me say this again; **none of these doctrines are to be found in the Book of Mormon. They aren't found in the Bible either**. The resulting conclusion is obvious. Either the Book of Mormon does NOT contain the fullness of the Latter-day Saints Gospel; or this book is Scripture and the Mormon church is false.

UNKNOWN LANGUAGE

It is claimed that the Gold Plates were written in ***"Reformed Egyptian."*** No scholar has yet been able to identify such a language. When we consider that the Lamanites were supposed to be Semitic or Jewish, why would they write in Egyptian, which was an accursed language to Hebrews/Jews? If the Book of Mormon was really written around 400AD, as is claimed, how can it be explained that so much of it was written in 1611 King James English - over 1,000 years prior to this style of language being spoken or written? Languages change and evolve; spelling, writing style and word meanings change over time. Most historic documents are dated by this method.

How can it also be explained that ***"adieu,"*** a French word, is recorded in Jacob 7:27? (This is dated by Mormon authorities at 544BC to 421BC.) The French language didn't exist until approximately 700AD!

The inscription was claimed to be on thin gold plates which had engravings on both sides. This is very difficult to either do or read. Gold weighs 1204.7 pounds per cubic foot. The plates were 7 x 8 x 6 inches. They would weigh about 234 pounds or 106 kilograms - about the same as a muscular adult human male. Yet Smith claimed to carry the plates around under his arm , and at one time he ran at least three miles with them while fighting off three robbers at the same time.[51] Shades of Samson, or an enhanced imagination?

THE SMITHSONIAN REPORT

The Mormon Church headquarters had been claiming that the Smithsonian Institute was using the Book of Mormon as a research tool. The Smithsonian finally released a report about this false claim.

"1/. The Smithsonian Institution has never used the Book of Mormon in any way as a scientific guide. Smithsonian archeologists see no direct connection between the archeology of the New World and the subject matter of the book.

2/. The physical type of the American Indian is basically Mongoloid, being most closely related to that of the peoples of eastern, central and northeastern Asia. Archeological evidence indicates that the ancestors of the present Indians came into the New World - probably over a land bridge known to have existed in the Bering Strait region during the last Ice Age - in a continuing series of small migrations beginning from about 25,000 to 30,000 years ago.

3/. Present evidence indicates that the first people to reach this continent from the East were the Norsemen who arrived in the northeastern part of North America around A.D. 1,000. There is nothing to show that they reached Mexico or Central America.

4/. One of the main lines of evidence supporting the scientific finding that contacts with Old World civilizations, if indeed they occurred at all, were of very little significance for the development of American Indian civilizations, is the fact that none of the principal Old World domesticated food plants or animals (except the dog) occurred in the New World in pre-Columbian times. American Indians had no wheat, barley, oats, millet, rice, cattle, pigs, chickens, horses, donkeys, camels etc., before 1492. The domesticated dogs of the Indians accompanied their ancestors from northwestern Asia. Domesticated sweet potatoes occurred in both hemispheres, but probably originated in the New World and spread from there into the Pacific.

5/. Iron, steel, glass and silk were not used in the New World before 1492 (except for occasional use of unsmelted meteoric iron). Nuggets of native copper were used in various locations in pre-Columbian times, but true metallurgy was limited to southern Mexico and the Andean region, where its occurrence in late prehistoric times involved gold, silver, copper and their alloys, but not iron.

6/. There is a possibility that the spread of cultural traits across the Pacific to Mesoamerica and the northwestern coast of South America began several hundred years before the Christian era. However, such inter-hemispheric contacts appear to have been the results of accidental voyages originating in eastern and southern Asia. It is by no means certain that even such contacts occurred; certainly there were no contacts with the ancient Egyptians, Hebrew, or other peoples of Western Asia and the Near East.

7/. No reputable Egyptologist or other specialist on Old World archeology, and no expert in New World prehistory, has discovered or confirmed any relationship between archeological remains in Mexico and archeological remains in Egypt.

8/. Reports of findings of ancient Egyptian, Hebrew and other Old World writings in the New World in pre-Columbian contexts have frequently appeared in newspapers, magazines and sensational books. None of these claims has stood up to examination by reputable scholars. No inscriptions using Old World forms of writing have been shown to have occurred in any part of the Americas before 1492." [20]

SCIENTIFIC CONCLUSIONS

Please read this carefully: No person, place, nation, or name from the Book of Mormon has ever been found! No artifact, gold plate or document has been produced to demonstrate that the Book of Mormon is anything other than a work of fiction. Why are there no maps in the Book of Mormon? The holy books of most religions have maps as part of their claim to authenticity.

North American Indians speak 169 related languages which stem from five language stocks. However, everyone in the Book of Mormon speaks only one language, claimed to be ***"Reformed Egyptian."***

With regard to point two above, anthropologists and genetic experts insist that native American Indians are related to the peoples of eastern, central and northeastern Asia. These Asian people have what is called a "Mongoloid Spot" a blue-gray spot which appears on their tailbone at birth. North American Indians have this same spot. The Israelites, who are Semitic, do not have this spot.

The Bureau of American Ethnology asserts there is no evidence of any Jewish migration to America before Columbus, and no evidence the Indians had any knowledge of the Bible or the Christian faith prior to 1492.

The National Geographic Society has also stated publicly they see nothing useful in the Book of Mormon to assist their work, and have found no evidence to support it. These are organisations whose scientific work has been thorough, independent and completely beyond question. The Book of Mormon is not just in trouble - it is effectively disproved by independent investigators and experts who have no axe to grind.

The archeological evidence for the Bible's people and places have led many archeologists, such as Sir William Ramsey, to become Christians because the evidence supporting the Bible record is so overwhelming. However the failure to locate even one scrap of evidence to support the Book of Mormon resulted in prominent Mormon archeologist, Thomas Stewart Ferguson, quitting the church of the Latter-day Saints and repudiating its prophet as false. This must have been quite a blow to Ferguson, as he had founded the "New World Archeological Foundation" for the express purpose of authenticating the Book of Mormon. Ferguson died around 1990.

If God is the author of both the Book of Mormon and the Bible, why does He not supply the same kind of evidence for the Book of Mormon which He has for the Bible? [21]

THE THREE WITNESSES

One fascinating thing about the Book of Mormon is the issue of "The Three Witnesses." Even today every copy of the Book of Mormon has a testimony allegedly signed by Oliver Cowdery, David Whitmer and Martin Harris attesting to having seen the gold plates. What is the truth?

Oliver Cowdery

Harris was excommunicated from the LDS church in 1837. He later testified publicly that he saw the gold plates with ***"The eyes of faith, and not the natural eyes."***[22] That means he never saw them! Whitmer formed one of the many breakaway groups, declaring himself to be the new prophet, and was excommunicated. Whitmer also publicly stated that he never saw the gold plates.[23]

Cowdery was the church's Second Elder, scribe to the Book of Mormon and present at the claimed restoration of the priesthood. In 1838 in Kirtland, Cowdery confronted his cousin, Joseph Smith Jnr., and accused him of adultery with Fanny Alger and also with lying and teaching false doctrines. For this Cowdery was excommunicated. Official church records show that Fanny Alger was Smith's first 'Spiritual Wife.' This was the beginning of polygamy in the Mormon Church. It didn't please the first Mrs. Smith. Later Cowdery became a Christian and publicly confessed his sorrow and shame at his involvement with Smith and Mormonism. He also stated emphatically he never once saw the gold plates.[24a] ***"The records show that he (Cowdery) and his family joined the Methodist Protestant Church in Tiffin, Ohio, about 1841, where Oliver served as secretary. When he died in 1850, he was buried by a Methodist minister, John Sexsmith, in Richmond, Missouri."***[24] There is no independent evidence that Cowdery ever rejoined the Mormon Church, despite claims by Mormons. If he had, why did a Methodist minister bury him?

Of the eleven witnesses listed in the front of the Book of Mormon, only the three Smiths (Joseph's father and two brothers) stayed with the Mormon Church. All three of the major witnesses are on public record saying the gold plates were a hoax. Yet all three are falsely held up to this day by the Mormon Church leaders as honoured witnesses. What they really witnessed was a fraud.

WHERE DID THE BOOK OF MORMON COME FROM?

Brigham Roberts

Mormon General Authority and apologist, Brigham H. Roberts, published a major research manuscript in 1922, entitled "The Book of Mormon Difficulties," and claimed that Joseph Smith Jnr. could well have authored the Book of Mormon himself.[25a] Roberts also wrote in his second manuscript, ***"Is all this sober history... or is it a wonder-tale of an immature mind, unconscious of what a test he is laying on human credulity when asking men to accept his narrative as solemn history?"***[25]

I have located other reasonable and logical explanations for the Book of Mormon. Young Joseph Smith's Sunday school teacher, a Congregational minister named Rev. Solomon Spaulding, used to write what he termed romances or fictional stories. He wrote at least two about Jesus visiting America after His resurrection. In view of Smith's known moral behaviour it seems likely that young Joe may have 'borrowed' a copy of Spaulding's manuscript, added over 27,000 words from the Bible of his day, plus some of his own fanciful prophecies, and then published it as his own work, divinely inspired of course! There is also a claim that Sidney Rigdon may have found Spaulding's manuscript in a publisher's office, and then taken it to Smith. Yet another possible source is Ethan Smith's manuscript, "View of the Hebrews." Ethan was not related to Joseph. Whichever is the true source, the Book of Mormon still doesn't quite qualify as the inspired Word of God, does it?[26]

It may be helpful to know that Spaulding's original manuscript has been compared with the Book of Mormon, so that source is quite easy to prove. Spaulding's granddaughter, who is now in her nineties, was on an American television programme in 1992 showing an original manuscript in her possession to prove this. There is a duplicate copy in the Oberlin College library, Ohio, which shows at least 75 distinctive similarities to the historic portions of the Book of Mormon.

IS MORMONISM CHRISTIAN?

By now any reader who attends a Mormon Church is likely to be angry. You should be too! You might be angry towards me because you think I have maligned your prophet and your holy book. But hold on a minute - what I have written here is public record and proven fact. I haven't made this up, and I don't have to. I am interested in the truth, to reveal the facts - the rest I leave to God. The evidence against both Smith and the Book of Mormon is overwhelming. I must question the integrity of many Mormon leaders who have deliberately misled - yes, lied - to their own people. Christians do not oppose Mormons, but we must oppose all teaching which claims to be Christian but which fails the Bible tests.

You thought the Latter Day Saints church was a Christian organisation, but it never has been. Dr. Anthony Hoekema, author of "The Four Major Cults," writes, ***"Mormonism does not deserve to be called a Christian religion. It is basically anti-Christian and anti-Biblical."***[27]

Gordon Fraser, author of four books on Mormonism, explains, ***"We object to Mormon missionaries posing as Christians, and our objections are based on the differences between what they are taught by the [Mormon] General Authorities and what the Bible teaches."***[28]

Probably the world's foremost expert on cults, Dr. Walter Martin, writes ***"In no uncertain terms the Bible condemns the teachings of the Mormon church."***[29]

These are strong words, and because they come from three of the most respected modern Christian experts on Mormonism, we need to check out the facts. No one denies that the average Mormon is a good citizen, thrifty, a good worker, well behaved, has a social conscience, and is hospitable and friendly. Missionaries knocking on your door will often make a major thing of the importance of family life. That's wonderful. There are good living and moral people in every religion, as well as atheism, so clearly good living isn't enough.

I was concerned to be told that between 75% and 85% of Mormons are not good enough to get a "Temple Recommend," which enables them to visit one of their temples and participate in the various ceremonies. I would point out that every Christian Church is open to all who wish to go to them. It should also be mentioned that Mormon Temple ceremonies are not found in the Bible, and are in fact condemned in the Book of Mormon in Ether 8:19. Jesus Christ said **"I spoke openly to the world... in secret I have said nothing,"** (John 18:20). If the Mormon Temple ceremonies are so good, they should not be kept secret. Claiming these are sacred so they should also be kept secret will not do. That they are kept from the majority of Mormons can only make us suspicious. I have read through the Mormon ceremonies and noted many similarities with those practised by the Masonic Lodges which I have also studied. My main comment would be that Bible-believing Christians have a serious problem with the spiritualist/pagan themes running through both organisations' ceremonies.

Mormon Apostle Orson Pratt state: ***"Who is the great whore of Babylon? It is the Catholic Church and her Protestant daughter who have defiled the earth with their filthiness and fornications."***[30] Mormons, along with everyone else, are entitled to believe in anything they wish. However it would be dishonest to label Mormonism "Christian" when many similar attacks, such as the one above, are delivered with considerable venom by Joseph Smith, Brigham Young, Orson Pratt and virtually every president and apostle of the Mormon church since. It seems Mormon leaders have no kind and gracious words for Christian leaders, but regard as persecution any truth-seeking investigation from others. This shows the double standard used by the Mormon General Authorities.

Just prior to completing this book, some Mormon leaders sent me a rather fascinating book by Mormon apologist and Brigham Young University professor, Stephen E. Robinson, entitled *"Are Mormons Christians?"* Anyone lacking the sort of factual information which I have included in this book (and especially the terms charts on pages 41-42) could be convinced that Mormons are indeed Christians. However, if we put aside the rose-coloured spectacles and read Robinson's book with the terms chart of Mormon redefinitions mentioned above, we can quickly see the Christianity Robinson writes about is not Bible-based: therefore it is not Christianity at all. Theologian Gordon Lewis is right when he says that Robinson's approach to legitimising Mormonism ***"can only succeed if a Christian does not need to believe in one personal, transcendent God, one incarnate Christ, the completed atonement, and one gospel of grace through faith alone.*** *(But Christians do believe these.)* ***Historians may classify every group that calls itself 'Christian' as Christian. Jesus Christ, however, did not do this. Jesus taught that 'the way' was narrow and that we should not assume that all who call Jesus 'Lord' are really Christians. (Matthew 5:20; 7:13-23.)"*** [31]

CHRISTIAN CONCERNS

Christians have not attacked the Mormon Church, but they do have the right and the authority of God to defend the Bible-based teaching of the Christian Church, as well as to challenge false teachers, false prophets and counterfeit saviours wherever these arise. ***"All cults embrace one or more of the following tenets: they either humanise God, deify man, minimise sin, or ostracise the Scriptures. Mormonism uses all four of these tenets to bring forth false doctrine."***[32] It is the issues of beliefs, doctrine and worship practices which cause Christians to be deeply concerned about Mormonism. Mormons believe that God regards the Christian worship of Him as unacceptable and offensive. Also the Mormons believe that there was a great apostasy from the time of the early church until Joseph Smith was given the task to restore the true doctrines, teachings and practices of God. This brings an irrevocable division between Christians and Mormons. Either one or the other may be right, but they are mutually exclusive of the other. Mormonism can never be regarded as another form of Christianity.

Christians are gravely concerned that Mormonism has turned aside to **"another Gospel, another Jesus and another Spirit,"** (2 Corinthians 11:4). Mormonism, as presently taught, is basically pagan polytheism, with a strong dose of Spiritualism, and is remarkably similar to Hinduism. Why should anyone believe it is Christian? Using Christian terminology is not enough, as we see on pages 41-42.

WHO IS GOD?

Joseph Smith taught, ***"In the Beginning, the head of the gods called a council of the gods; and they came together and concocted a plan to create the world and people it."***[33] He also said, ***"God himself was once as we are now, and is an exalted man."***[34] Prophet Lorenzo Snow wrote, ***"As man is, God once was; as God is, man may become."***[35] ***"The Father has a body of flesh and bones as tangible as man's, the Son also."***[36] Brigham Young taught that Adam was God, and Eve was only one of his many goddess wives.[37] (In fact, there are 48 official Mormon volumes which state that Adam was God and also the Father of Jesus.) These are just a few of many similar official writings and statements, so they are in context.

But what does the Bible say? **"Hear, O Israel: the LORD our God, the LORD is one,"** (Deuteronomy 6:4). **"You believe that there is one God. You do well. Even the demons believe - and tremble,"** (James 2:19). **"Besides Me there was no God formed, nor shall there be after Me. I, even I, am the LORD, and besides Me there is no saviour,"** (Isaiah 43:10b-11a). **"Thus says the LORD,...I am the First and I am the Last; besides Me there is no God,... Is there a God besides Me?... I know not one,"** (Isaiah 44:6,8). **"God is Spirit, and those who**

worship Him must worship in spirit and in truth," (John 4:24). Jesus said, **"...a spirit does not have flesh and bones..."** (Luke 24:39).

What does all this mean? The Mormon leaders are saying that God is an evolving man, and we can be gods too. In his last recorded sermon just prior to his death, Joseph Smith challenged his people to learn to become gods. This is a Hindu belief now being adopted by many New Age spiritualists. The only Biblical source for this idea is found in Genesis 3:5, where the Serpent/Satan suggested it. The God of the Bible says that apart from Him the only other gods are false ones. I don't want to know those gods, for their purpose is to deceive and hurt us. There is only one true God, and He reserves divinity for Himself exclusively. Mormon men who plan to becomes gods are in for a big disappointment - there are no vacancies in the Godhead, for the position is already taken and He has no plans to share it! The Mormon doctrine of God raises some heavy questions which Mormon leaders can't answer. If God was once a man, how did he learn to evolve into a god? Who created the first man, or woman if all the gods evolved from men?

I have heard Mormons emphatically claim that God was once a man, and they boldly state that the Bible confirms this. They quote Scriptures which speak of God's hand, God's eye, God's ear and God's footstool, etc. Unfortunately these poor people have been taught by leaders who have missed the point of these Scriptures, namely that God hears every word we speak, that He sees everything we do, and that He is involved in His creation. Psalm 91:4 invites us to shelter under God's wings and amongst His feathers. Are the Mormons teaching that God is a turkey or a hen? That is absurd. Jesus describes Himself as the "Bread of Life" and as a door. That doesn't imply Jesus is a loaf of cooked dough, or wood and hinges. The language is figurative. How else could we understand what He means when God calls Himself **"A Consuming Fire?"** Is He now a blast furnace? Of course not. He is speaking of His divine judgement which He will bring onto those who rebel against His will as revealed in the Bible.

Think about it for a moment. If we are totally honest we have to admit not one of us has the patience or the love to put up with mankind the way God has chosen to. We would have wiped them all out in our anger, and started again. Who could blame God for even thinking that? However a gracious and merciful God, because of His great love for us, paid the penalty for sin Himself on Calvary, so our relationship might be restored to Him. There is a huge difference between our Creator and us creatures. We can never be like Him!

The facts are plain. When one considers the Mormon concept of God and alongside it compares the Biblical Christian concept of God, we cannot be looking at ***'different views of one God'*** - we are looking at ***'views of different Gods.'*** There is nothing in common.

DOCTRINAL DIFFERENCES

I quoted above three leading Christian authors who are cult experts and who object to Mormons posing as Christians on the basis of the Bible's teaching. Space limitations prevents a deeper look into these issues so I will briefly cover only a few of the major doctrines. Let us compare the latest official Mormon teaching with the biblical Christian teaching.[38]

Mormonism	***Christianity***
	The Bible
Unreliable	*Proven reliable*
Incomplete	*The complete Word of God*
Requires new revelations	*New revelations forbidden by Bible*
	The Nature of God
Polytheistic (many gods)	*Monotheistic/trinity (3 persons in 1 God)*
Evolved man	*Always God*
Physical & finite	*Spirit and infinite*
Morally imperfect	*Eternally Holy*
(Required salvation)	*(Sinless)*
Sexual Polygamist	*Non-sexual*
	Jesus
Created Being	*Eternally God*
Exalted to godhood	*Never required exaltation*
Earned salvation	*Never required salvation - holy*
Conceived by sex (between	*Conceived by the Holy Spirit*
Mary & Adam or Elohim)	*(overshadowing true virgin, Mary)*
Married polygamist	*Unmarried celibate*
	Salvation
Works required	*God's grace alone*
Christ's sacrifice insufficient	*Atoning sacrifice at Calvary total*
Required to shed own blood	*Jesus did it all*
You can be saved after death	*Only Judgement after death*
	After Death
Celestial heaven	*Eternal heaven*
(for good Mormons)	*(Dwelling place of God)*
Terrestrial heaven	*Eternal hell*
(good non-Mormons & those	*(Wicked {those who reject God}*
accepting Mormonism after death)	*(are punished there forever)*
Telestial heaven (for wicked)	*No purgatory or evolving after death*

Christians have the Bible, which is the Word of God, and against which all teaching and lifestyle must be measured. Mormons believe their Presidents are seers and prophets. The leaders claim to have "progressive revelation," which means they are able to replace a belief or teaching which gets embarrassing. That is neither progressive or revelation, even if it is convenient. It does prove that the God of the Bible cannot be the source of their revelations. Jesus said that heaven and earth would pass away before a single word of his failed (Matthew 5:18), and the Father confirms this **"The grass withers and the flower fades, but the word of our God stands forever,"** (Isaiah 40:8).

THE MORMON PLAN OF ETERNAL PROGRESSION

The Mormon Church teaches:

1. We exist eternally as an "intelligence" (box 1). We progress to a pre-mortal spirit world (box 2). God and one of his wives begat us as a spirit. (Mormons teach God is an exalted man of flesh and bone, so why beget spiritual children and not physical ones?)

2. Other spirit offspring of God and his wives include Jesus and Lucifer. Because Lucifer lost the vote to Jesus at the Council of gods about who would become saviour of planet Earth, Lucifer attempted the first rebellion and was expelled from heaven, along with those spirits who supported him. These spirits are denied a physical body.

3. The good spirits who fought with Jesus in the battle were given the best bodies on earth - these have white skins. Those who were neutral in the fight were still given bodies, but these had black skins.

4. After death those who didn't accept Mormonism go to a spirit prison (box 4), and are given further teaching by Mormon spirit missionaries. Those who reject Mormonism are resurrected for judgement (no. 5). Wicked humans are sent to the Telestial Kingdom (box 7), while the rebellious spirits who never had bodies are sent to the Second Death (box 6).

5. Those who accept Mormonism on earth go to Paradise (box 4a) and are later resurrected at the Millennium, and proceed to positive judgement and blessing.

6. Good living and religious people who still reject Mormonism are sent to the Terrestrial Kingdom (box 8).

7. Those who accepted Mormonism are elevated to the Celestial Kingdom (box

The Mormon Plan of Eternal Progression

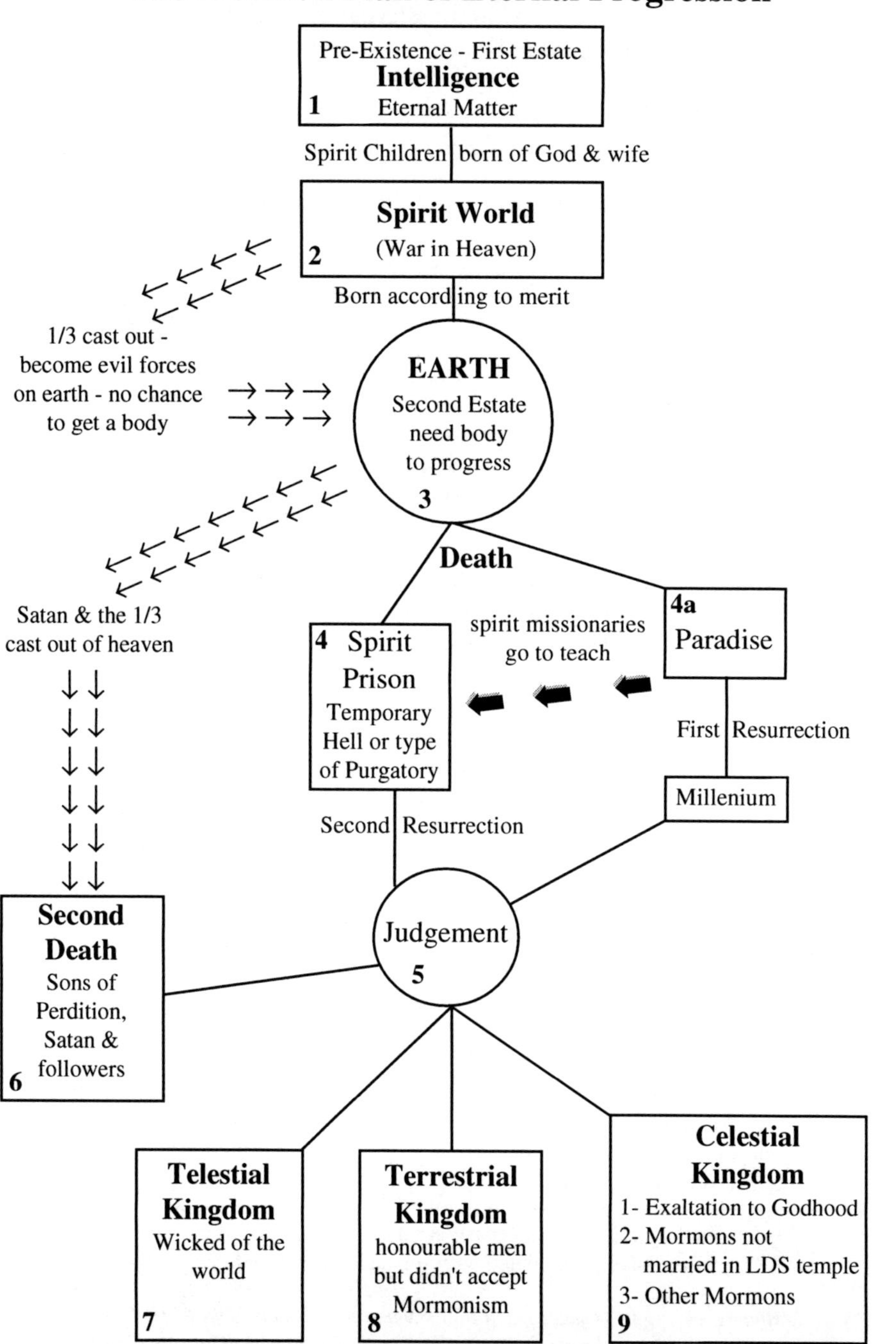

THE BIBLE TEACHES US
God the Eternal
(revealed as Father, Son & Holy Spirit)

↓

Earth & inhabitants & angels created

↓

Rebellion in heaven - Lucifer & 1/3rd of angels expelled

↓

Adam & Eve sin, deceived by Lucifer/Satan.
Result = relationship with God broken.
Nothing repairs break - not animal sacrifices, the Law, the Temple.

↓

Emmanuel - "God with Us" - God the Son puts on a body of flesh.
After ministry & teaching for 3 1/2 years, Jesus crucified at Calvary.
The true sacrifice for all sin.

✞✞✞

Jesus resurrected 3 days later,
40 days later ascended to heaven with many eyewitnesses.

↓

Pentecost 10 days later, Believers empowered by Holy Spirit.
Result = evangelism, faith in Jesus & repentence of sin,
even with occasional division & deceptions of some parts of the church.

When people die

The physical body disintegrates (burial or cremation).
↓ The spirit goes to God & the soul goes to one of two places. ↓

 Those who reject Jesus & did not repent of sin go to Hades (Death Row) to await Judgement Day.	Those who believe in Jesus Christ & repent of sin go to Paradise to await Judgement Day. 

↓ On Judgement Day, everyone will be resurrected,
rejoining their body with their spirit & the soul. ↓

☹ Those whose names are not in The Book of Life had pre-chosen to join Lucifer & his fallen angels in Hell, the place of eternal torment. *(Rev. 20:10,15)*	Those whose names are recorded in The Book of Life *(Rev. 21:27)* are admitted into God's eternal presence. 

The physical heavens & earth are then destroyed because
they have been tainted with sin, and are replaced. *(Rev. 21:1)*

(Matters relating to Armageddon, the Millennium etc. don't affect the facts of the two eternal destinations following Judgement Day, so have been left out for space reasons.)

9). Polygamy, paying tithes on time and loyalty to Mormon leadership are the main criteria for exaltation to godhood. Women may only become goddesses if their husbands call them forth. The other two levels in the Celestial Kingdom are for less zealous Mormons. It is interesting the Book of Mormon fails to mention these three heavens (represented in boxes 7, 8 & 9). Let me explain there is no Biblical basis to these Mormon beliefs, including those shown in the chart on page 27. The primary source for this information is official Mormon material.[55]

God's Word, the Bible, presents a totally different view (see chart page 28). We are created by God only when our parents have a physical relationship. We are spiritual beings who have souls (wills and emotions), and during our physical lifetime we inhabit a body. Your spirit and soul is the real you and does not exist prior to conception, but will continue to exist forever. While our bodies are alive we must decide to accept or reject Jesus Christ, for He is the sole source of salvation. After our physical death there are one of two places to spend eternity - heaven, with Jesus; or hell, without Him. There is no movement between those places, according to Jesus in Luke 16:19-31. Jesus also explained there would not be marriage in heaven in Mark 12:25.

There are spiritual beings called "angels," who didn't preexist either but were created by God for special tasks. Angels do not have, nor need, physical bodies. Lucifer attempted a takeover of heaven and the universe, supported by one-third of the angels, but they were defeated by God and expelled from His presence. These fallen angels we call evil spirits or demons, and there are various ranks of importance. The evidence is very solid that Moroni is a senior fallen angel. The two-thirds of the angels who remained loyal to God are involved to worshipping God and fulfilling God's plans by involvement in human affairs, such as protecting believers. God doesn't make it up as He goes along - He has an ultimate plan He is working to, and which is happening on perfect schedule.

FAMILIAR SPIRITS

When the Mormon missionaries call, they often attempt to give people a copy of the Book of Mormon. Let's get to the point; ask them if they believe there is a Familiar Spirit with the book. If they are honest (and informed) they should answer ***"Yes."***[39] Since this is true, you have every right to decline to have it in your home, on the basis of the following Scriptures;

"Give no regard to mediums and familiar spirits, do not seek after them to be defiled by them: I am the LORD your God," (Leviticus 19:31).

"...the person who turns after mediums and familiar spirits, to prostitute himself with them, I will set My face against that person and cut him off from his people," (Leviticus 20:6).

"A man or a woman who is a medium, or who has familiar spirits, shall surely be put to death..," (Leviticus 20:27). (See also Deuteronomy 18:9-12, Isaiah 29:4 and Galatians 6:19-21.)

There are fifteen Old Testament references to familiar spirits, and all of them refer to mediums involved in witchcraft. If the Mormon Church believes that every Book of Mormon has its own familiar spirit, they are choosing to identify with witchcraft. A medium is someone on friendly terms with a familiar spirit or demon. The primary purpose of the familiar spirit which accompanies the Book of Mormon is to deceive you. No person who is genuinely seeking the God of the Bible would willingly invite a deceiving demon into their home. (This matter is dealt with in greater detail in another book in this series, "Unmasking Spiritualism.")

FEELINGS OR FAITH?

The Mormon missionaries at your door will also often invite you to pray to their heavenly father as to whether Mormonism, the Book of Mormon and Joseph Smith are all true. They will tell you that if you do this you will experience a ***"burning in the Bosom."*** This is the manifestation of the deceiving spirit, and should not be prayed for. Mormons have misunderstood the Scripture in Luke 24:13 about a similar experience which the disciples did not have to pray for, the source of which was the true God and not a familiar spirit.

When faced with the false teachings of Mormonism, a Mormon will almost always say to you, ***"I testify to you, I know the Book of Mormon is true. I know Joseph Smith was a prophet of God. I know the Mormon Church is true and its President is a prophet on the earth today."*** Because of the form of brainwashing or mind control involved, this statement becomes a sort of self-hypnosis of confirmation, because if these statements are false (which they are) then that person's faith is lost, and the person would be understandably devastated. If you ask, ***"How do you know these things are true?"*** They will probably tell you the Holy Ghost has manifested these things to them when they have prayed. In other words, they got a "feeling" from a deceiving familiar spirit. Mormons make a big thing of "feelings," but the Bible teaches otherwise. Christians are told **"Do not believe every spirit, but test the spirits, whether they are of God; because many false prophets have gone out into the world,"** (1 John 4:1). Other Scriptures (including 1 Thessalonians 5:21 and Acts 17:11) repeat God's challenge for us to be sure on spiritual matters. Some Mormc deceased relative has appeared to them, telling them that the Mori true. The Bible is specific that dead people cannot do that. As Dr. says, ***"Dead relatives cannot visit!"*** (See Luke 16:19-21.) What a familiar spirit who knew about the relative when they were alive.

A Christian should respond thus: **"Your personal testimony is actually invalid because I testify to you that Joseph Smith was a false prophet, the Mormon Church is not true, Jesus Christ is my Lord and Saviour, the President of the Mormon Church is not a prophet of God on this earth today, and I say this in the name of Jesus Christ."** Your testimony is just as valid as the Mormon's, and in fact more so, because it is true. Spiritual truth is never based on someone's testimony, but on the objective Word of God. It isn't what we think that really matters - it is what God says in the Bible.

THE PRIESTHOODS

Joseph Smith claimed to restore the original doctrines of the Christian church, including the priesthoods of Aaron and Melchizedek. Membership of these priesthoods is claimed as the God-given authority to do every important function in the Mormon Church. So where do these priesthoods come from? On May 15, 1829, Joseph Smith and Oliver Cowdery baptised and ordained each other into the Aaronic Priesthood, claiming that John the Baptist had visited them under the instructions of the Apostles, Peter, James and John. Sometime in the following six weeks, these three Apostles are alleged to have visited Smith and conferred on him the Melchizedek Priesthood.

Mormon theology teaches that every person must be baptised by someone with authority to baptise, in other words someone who has themselves already received a proper authentic baptism. Otherwise the baptism is invalid. Since Joseph Smith Jnr. had not himself been baptised when he received the Aaronic Priesthood,[40] by what authority did he baptise Cowdery on May 15, 1829? Cowdery was then improperly baptised, so he also lacked the authority to baptise Smith later the same day. Mormons cannot ignore the staggering consequences of this. By the official declarations of the Mormon Church leadership, because neither Cowdery nor Smith were authentically baptised in the first place, not a single Mormon since 1829 has yet received an authentic baptism: all are invalid by their Church's declarations. Because Mormons claim that baptism is necessary for salvation, their salvation is also invalid. Because of this terrible oversight by their leadership back to 1829, no Mormon can be assured of anything - their baptism, their salvation, or anything else.

.. LDS Aaronic Priesthood has three degrees, Deacon, Teacher and Priest. The LDS Melchizedek Priesthood has five degrees, Elder, Seventies, High Priest, Patriarch and Apostle. Let us investigate these further.

The Bible is clear that to belong to the priestly order of Aaron requires one to be born into the Tribe of Levi. Number 3:10 limits the Aaronic Priesthood to Aaron, his sons, and their direct descendents. Numbers 18:7 goes further and states that anyone other than Levites who came near the sanctuary were to be put to death. So every member of the ***"Aaronic Priesthood"*** is claiming to be a Levite by physical birth and inheritance. But there is a problem. When Jerusalem was sacked by the Romans in 70AD all the lineage records were destroyed. No one has been able to prove his tribal lineage since then, including Joseph Smith. Tribal lineage and ancestry have always been important to Israelite/Jewish people. Mormons have picked up on this practice, somewhat imperfectly. The Mormon Book of Abraham claims that Egyptians were cursed and couldn't hold any priesthoods.[41] Joseph Smith claims his family lineage is from the tribe of Ephraim.[42] and that Book of Mormon people were from the tribe of Manasseh.[43] Both Ephraim and Manasseh were the sons of Joseph (son of Jacob) and Asenath. Since Asenath was an Egyptian (Genesis 41:45, 50), Ephraim and Manasseh were both half-caste Egyptians, and so were disqualified from any priesthood. If Joseph Smith's family line were truly from Ephraim, he could never validly hold any priesthood office.

The original Aaronic/Levitical Priesthood were divinely commanded to perform ceremonial washing, slaying of bullocks for sacrifice, the sprinkling of their blood for atonement, then burning the sacrifice, followed by seven days separation from other people and activities. If the Mormon Aaronic Priesthood is truly 'restored' where have these functions gone? Are those Mormons who think they are members of the Aaronic priesthood still sacrificing animals to God? If it were so important, why is the Aaronic priesthood not even mentioned in the Book of Mormon? There are two other important considerations; Jesus Himself could not belong to the Aaronic Priesthood since He came from the tribe of Judah, not Levi. Also Jesus Christ abolished the Aaronic Priesthood with His sacrificial death at Calvary, since He was the perfect and acceptable sacrifice to God the Father, (see Hebrews 7:11-19; & 8:6-13.)

The Mormon ***"Melchizedek Priesthood"*** is also interesting. The Book of Mormon only records this order once, and states it belongs only to Melchizedek. If the Book of Mormon is the "Fullness of the Gospel," then what use are priesthoods it doesn't teach? The LDS Melchizedek Priesthood claims the authority to preach the Gospel, to baptise and to offer sacraments. There is no basis in either the Bible or the Book of Mormon for these activities. Hebrews 7:24 states that this order is the peculiar, exclusive and permanent possession of Jesus Christ. The Greek word used is "*aparabatos,*" which means "untransferable," and literally means "without successors." Jesus would not and could not share or transfer this order to anyone else. Since Jesus Christ is the exclusive owner and member of this priesthood, (especially since New Testament times) what actually has been restored? The meaning is obvious! Any person who claims to belong to the Melchizedek Priesthood is actually claiming to be Jesus Christ. *(This also applies to the 19th Degree of Scottish Rite Freemasonry.)* If that is you, then please provide your credentials to be Israel's Messiah and the Saviour of the world. If you can't then I recommend quick repentance for such blasphemy.

The Mormon Church claim that Peter, James and John ordained Joseph Smith into this priestly order. Since it was never theirs to give, this too is invalid. Hebrews 7:1-3, and 26-27 record the qualifications for the Melchizedek Priesthood. Who is "**holy, harmless, undefiled, separate from sinners, and made higher than the heavens**?" Only Jesus Christ! None of us can ever possess this priesthood, or the authority claimed for it by the Mormon Church.

Mormons have a High Priestly order, but the only mention of High Priests in the New Testament involved the persecution of Jesus and the Christians. In a nutshell, the Mormon priesthoods are worthless as far as God is concerned, and are quite misleading to those in them.

In 1832 Smith claimed to have a revelation which stated that a man could only see God if he had received the Mormon priesthoods. If this were true, how can Smith claim he saw God in 1820, since the priesthoods weren't invented by Smith until May 15, 1829?[44] Also, why do Mormons use their priesthoods to communicate with the spirits of the dead when God specifically forbade such practices in Deut. 18:10-14 and Galatians 5:20? Both LDS Priesthood Orders remain invalid!

THE GENUINE PRIESTHOOD OF BELIEVERS

There is a genuine Biblical priesthood for Christians and according to 1 Peter 2:9-10 and Revelation 1:6, it is the priesthood of all believers in Jesus Christ. However by following the teaching of Joseph Smith the Mormons are actually left without a true Biblical priesthood. By denying the atoning sacrifice of Jesus Christ at Calvary, they prevent themselves from sharing in the priesthood of all believers. Christians have a High Priest after the order of Melchizedek, and His name is Jesus Christ. God promises that those who believe in Him, **"...to them He gave the right to become children of God..."** (John 1:12). The Bible allows women and children to belong to the priesthood of all believers, but the Mormon church forbids this. All other priesthoods were cancelled at Calvary, and God made sure by wiping them out when the Romans destroyed Jerusalem in 70 AD.

RESTORED OR SUBSTITUTED

As mentioned above, the Mormon Church teaches that Joseph Smith restored the true church and its practices. Mormon Apostles Roberts, Pratt and Talmage all claimed there was a universal or total apostasy for 1800 years until Joseph restored the church. Is that really true? The New Testament church had no First Presidency, no Patriarch, no High Priests, no Stake Presidencies and no Ward Bishoprics. How can you restore what never existed in the first place? Christ never excommunicated any of His twelve apostles; but Joseph Smith excommunicated six of his (Warren Parrish, John F. Boynton, Luke S. Johnson, Joseph Coe, William E. McLellin and William Smith). The Mormon Church actually has fifteen apostles, including the three in the First Presidency. Where did that number come from? Certainly not from the Bible.

Ephesians 3:21 speaks of **"the church of Christ Jesus throughout all ages..,"** while Jesus said **"...I will build my church and the gates of Hades will not prevail against it,"** (Matthew 16:18). He started with only twelve disciples, and now over one third of humanity claims Jesus Christ as Lord. Hebrews 7:24-25 shows Jesus lives forever, and Colossians 1:18 states that **"...He [Jesus] is the head of the body, the church..."** This is a present tense statement, so Jesus needs no successor, not even Joseph Smith. Christians have every right to ask Mormons to stop insulting the living Head of the Church, Jesus Christ, by questioning what sort of shepherd loses his flock for 1800 years. Jesus Christ has never stopped building His church.

It will be Jesus who will restore His church when He returns, **"Repent therefore and be converted, that your sins may be blotted out, so that times of refreshing may come from the presence of the Lord, and that He may send Jesus Christ, who was preached to you before, whom heaven must receive until the times of restoration of all things, which God has spoken by the mouth of all His holy prophets since the world began,"** (Acts 3:19-21). We established earlier that because the Mormon prophets had spoken falsely they could not be God's prophets, so this Scripture is not speaking of them but of the true and proven prophets of God. Claiming to be the one true church, as Mormon leaders do, does not make it so. The Mormon Jesus cannot save us because he is **"another Jesus,"** according to Galatians 1:8-9.

It is the Christ of the church which saves, not the church of Christ. Many have joined local churches of all labels, and remain without salvation, which can occur only when one becomes a member of the Body of Christ. (Please see Colossians 1:18,24; 1 Corinthians 12:27; Ephesians 1:22-23.) Regardless of the numbers, Jesus has true believers in every generation from His ascension until His return.

THE CROSS AND THE PERISHING

If Mormons really were Christians they would not reject the cross. Jesus said, **"And he who does not take up his cross and follow Me is not worthy of Me,"** (Matthew 10:38). (See also Matthew 16:24, Mark 8:34, 10:21, Luke 9:23, 14:27, Philippians 3:18-19.) Isn't it interesting that the Jehovah's Witnesses and the Mormons (probably the two most prominent cults in the world) both reject the Cross of Christ. It is the Word of God which judges such rejection. **"For the message of the cross is foolishness to those who are perishing, but to us who are being saved it is the power of God,"** (1 Corinthians 1:18). (See also Galatians 6:14, Philippians 2:7, Colossians 1:20-22, 2:14-15, Ephesians 2:15, Hebrews 12:12.)

The message of the Cross is central to the Christian faith, which explains why Paul wrote about it in almost every letter he sent to the early churches. Those who reject the Cross also reject the one whose blood was shed on it at Calvary.

Nowhere in the world is there a cross on top of a Mormon temple. Over two-thirds of the temples have on their spires a statue of the ***"Angel Moroni."*** (See below, and page 36.) Who is really being worshipped in these temples, Moroni or Jesus? God's angels can only bring messages which confirm God's teaching in the Bible, and they insist we worship and give glory to Jesus. Moroni brought teaching contrary to the Bible, so he can't be from God. There is only one other source: Satan. We are left with the inevitable conclusion that Moroni is a created spiritual being in rebellion to God and presently a senior prince in the hierarchy of Satan. His purpose has been to deceive, and he succeeded with Joseph Smith by bringing a gospel different from that of the Bible.

One of the major reasons for these temples is the Baptism for the Dead. It is one of the major reasons Mormons pursue genealogy studies, to they can baptise the dead by proxy and so enable them to be saved. ***"We are the only people that know how to save our progenitors, how to save ourselves, and how to save our posterity in the celestial kingdom of God; that we are the people God has chosen by whom to establish***

his kingdom and introduce correct principles into the world; and that we are in fact the saviours of the world..." wrote Prophet John Taylor.[45] That is a bold statement, even if it is untrue.

How do Mormons know that the dead person for whom proxy baptism is being performed has actually received the gospel message in the spirit world? The baptism would be invalid for any who reject the message. Since we cannot know if the dead person has received or rejected the message, to do it "just in case" is a charade, playing with ceremonies, no matter how well intentioned. 1 Timothy 1:4 and Titus 3:9 are Bible rejections of genealogy studies, described as **"unprofitable and useless."** 1 Corinthians 15:29 does not say that Baptism for the Dead was a Christian practice. There is no historic or Biblical evidence to suggest it ever was. In fact Paul is arguing for resurrection, not baptism.

"Nor is there salvation in any other, for there is no other name *(than Jesus Christ)* **under heaven given among men by which we must be saved,"** (Acts 4:12). John said, **"Behold the Lamb of God who takes away the sin of the world!"** (John 1:29). None of us can save ourselves, much less the dead or the world. Salvation comes through the repentance of sins by a person old enough and alive enough to do so, (thereby excluding minors, the dead, etc.) and putting our trust/faith in the person and promises of Jesus Christ.

WHY THE MASONIC CONNECTION?

I'm curious why in some Mormon temple ceremonies Lucifer wears an apron with Masonic symbols on it. When Adam asks what these are, Lucifer replies, ***"This is an emblem of my power and my priesthoods."***[46] Why are the temple endowments based on Masonic ceremonies? Because God rejected the apron (as a covering for sin) in the Garden of Eden, why would He reinstate it through Joseph Smith?

Occultic Comparisons

Mormon Priesthood	***Masonic equivalent***	***Penalty/Curse***
Aaronic - 1st Token	*1° Entered Apprentice*	*Having your throat cut & tongue torn out*
Aaronic - 2nd Token	*2° Fellow Craft*	*Having chest cut open & heart torn out*
Melchizedek - 1st Token	*3° Master Mason*	*Having stomach ripped open& entrails burned*

These oaths, penalties and signs are covered in some depth in my book, "Unmasking Freemasonry," and I don't wish to duplicate them here. However it is obvious these are mutilation and death curses from occultism and witchcraft, and are specifically forbidden by God in the Bible!

Why do the handgrips of the Aaronic priesthood exactly match the handgrips of Masonry's Blue Lodge? Why does a Mason being initiated into the Scottish Rite's 19th Degree have oil put on him after which he is told he is now ***"a priest forever after the order of Melchizedek?"*** (See page 31.) The compass & square used on the Mormon temple veil and the sacred undergarments are Masonic symbols (with a pagan significance) and have been for centuries, as are the handshakes through the veil. Because the Masons know all the signs, tokens and penalties, does that mean they will enter the Mormon celestial heaven? No Mormon leader has been able to provide a satisfactory answer to these many questions.

RACIAL DOCTRINE COVER-UP

Joseph Smith taught that people with darker skins were inferior and even cursed by God. Mixed-race marriages were forbidden. The excuse given was that in the

"Preexistence" the angels/spirits of those who didn't take sides in the battle between Jesus and Lucifer over who would be God of this world were cursed by God to have dark skins. ***"Negroes in this life are denied the priesthood; under no circumstances can they hold this delegation of authority from the Almighty. The gospel message of salvation is not carried affirmatively to them ...Negroes are not equal with other races where the receipt of certain spiritual blessings are concerned,"*** wrote Bruce R. McConkie, Mormon Apostle.[47] In summary, Mormon leaders taught that black skins were evidence of God's curse. On the other hand, the Bible records that God loves all human beings and He created them equal, (Genesis 1:26-28, John 3:16). This racist doctrine was only amended on June 9, 1978, to allow 'worthy' Negroes, Indians and others to hold the priesthoods and other privileges previously withheld from them. Again it was pressure from the American Government which forced Mormon leaders to receive a "new revelation" on this teaching.[48] Inquiries suggest it was the threat to withdraw government funding support for Mormon schools and universities which prompted this change of revelation. It appears some aspects of Mormon teaching are kept from some members, and this is a clear example. None of the New Zealand Maori or Pacific Island Mormons who I spoke with were aware of their church's past racist doctrines.

Research indicates that about one half of all New Zealand Mormon adherents are Maori, with Pacific Islanders making up another 20%. Pre-European Maori and Polynesian culture and religion included spiritualist ancestor worship and spirit communication. This remains a prominent aspect of Mormon teaching and practice, and obviously appeals today to many Maori and Polynesians seeking their cultural roots. Another likely factor is the desire to seek the salvation of their deceased relatives through proxy baptism for the dead - an admirable thought but a pointless action. The God of the Bible strongly condemns and forbids these practices (Deuteronomy 18:10-11, and Galatians 6:19-21). The Mormon church also claims about one-third of Tongans and one-quarter of Samoans as adherents, although these numbers are disputed by Pacific Island Christians and government census data. .

TESTIMONY OF "TONY,"
former L.D.S. Branch president

"In the mid 1970's we moved for business purposes to a new town, and we were basically loved into the Mormon Church. Our next door neighbour was a very outgoing person, and he used to visit us and I would notice he wouldn't eat anything on certain days of the month and he wouldn't drink alcohol with me and things like that. This generated a natural curiosity; he never actually promoted his faith or anything like that. But over a period of two or three months we got to understand he

was a Mormon, and we were invited out on car rallies, picnics with their family and other members of their church, and eventually it developed they sent some missionaries around to teach us, and we were asked to read the Book of Mormon and things like that. I remember quite distinctly one night in bed, I was thinking about it and a voice said quite clearly, "You've got no need to read this, you know that it's true." It was at that point I made a commitment to join the Latter Day Saints. With hindsight now, this is the trap and the danger of depending on feelings rather than scriptural content. We fell into a counterfeit church, and it wiped us out for a period of five or six years until we managed to come out again. Our whole family went in. There are lots of stories of splitting of families in the Mormon Church, but this didn't happen to us. We met lots of lovely kind people in the Mormon church, and we have got no argument with any of them at all. Our argument has ultimately come down to doctrine.

I was brought up in the Methodist church and attended Sunday School and Bible School until my late teens when we drifted away as we went into business and overseas. So when we came into the Latter-day Saints we came in without knowing much about it. My mother as well as all of our children joined and were taught the LDS doctrines. I eventually became appointed as a branch President in another town and served there for four years. I went through the various Temple ceremonies for time and eternity at the Mormon temple with our children and so on. Every so often I would come across a little bit which was a bit strange or unusual, and think "that's funny," Still you would sort of accept it. Then a couple of weeks later you would be taught something else, and think again "that's funny," and you would accept that. Over the years you accept degree by degree some things which you look back at the over all picture and it is absolutely absurd. But not knowing any better, and not knowing the Scriptures well we accepted these things, and so did our family.

During that time there was an Ex-Mormons for Jesus bookshop operating in Auckland, and they were sending lots of material out, and we received some. They were obviously mailing it to branch presidents and things like that, and we received it and I threw it into a draw, and never even opened it. It sat there for at least two years I suppose. One day, during the time we were in the LDS church, my mother became a temple worker in Hamilton and used to go there quite regularly and help with the temple ceremonies. I recall when we came out. It was one Saturday afternoon, and I suddenly thought to myself, "I wonder what was in that material?"

So I hunted it out from my bedroom draw, opened it up, and we decided to leave the church within about ten minutes of reading it, it was just like that. It was very dramatic. We saw material there where what affected me from an intellectual point of view was the letter from the chap Brown, who was a librarian in the LDS headquarters in Salt Lake, saying that some of the early revelations given to Joseph Smith had been changed. It was quite obvious as there were photocopies there to show the changes. There was another letter from one of the senior apostles in the LDS church saying the revelations of Joseph Smith had not been changed and that they stood forever. That was immediately and absolutely incontrovertible - you just couldn't deny the written evidence. So we had an immediate problem. Our teenage daughter had been studying the Book of Mormon for four years, along with seminary classes and things like this. My wife, and my five children, as well as my mother were all involved.

My mother was due to visit us on the way back from the temple that Saturday afternoon, and in fact while we were reading the material she actually knocked at the door, and it was quite spectacular as we were busy hiding it under the cushions and places like this, and my mother came and sat down on the couch, not knowing that underneath her was all this anti-Mormon material. However we had to do something about it. That Saturday night we had a meeting with all the Mormon folk in the town, so after about an hour of plucking up enough courage I said to Mum, "I don't believe the church is true - I have just seen evidence that it is not true." At the back of out mind was this fracture of families, it is just as hard to come out of the Mormon church as it is to get in. My mother just turned around and said, "Look, Anthony, if you don't believe it's true then that's it, finish!" And she was prepared to walk away, which absolutely amazed me.

We were a right mess that night. We told the children, and they were in tears. It was really quite a disastrous scene, there were tears everywhere, there was a complete and utter loss of faith, and so I knew we had to do something. There was one particular minister in the town that I had particular respect for from my business dealings with him, so we rang him up and he said later on he was as nervous as could be and didn't know what he was getting into to, but initially he said he had a meeting that night and couldn't make it, but he rang back about ten minutes later and said he would be happy to come out and see us. He came out to our house, about ten miles out in the country, it was really just a comforting exercise, because in the Mormon scene you are taught that the Book of Mormon is true and it is the only true religion on the earth. So when folk come out you tend to be completely disillusioned and say, well, if Mormonism isn't true then none of the churches are true, because that is the basis it exists on.

So we had to be convinced again that there was life after Mormonism, and he was there from about seven in the evening until about half- past eleven, and we were firing questions at him, and he was very politely saying, "Well, I don't think it quite says that in the Bible." We were very very confused, but from there we went on and we never for a moment considered not joining a mainstream church. We went to the Baptist Fellowship and I eventually became treasurer there for a number of years. So, we have had an exciting time I suppose, and I do look back on there Mormon era of our lives and it seems to be a time where we stagnated really, and it has taken a long time to overcome that. Our family is still together and they are all Christians and it is great.

When I look back in retrospect, although the Holy Spirit is acknowledged in Mormonism, I never actually saw him active, and I don't just say that in hindsight. In the Mormon church you sit down to sing your hymns, and little things like that which seems to strangle the outpouring of the Spirit, and you can't even talk about it in the same breath, because Mormonism is a counterfeit, so any spirit that is there has got to be a counterfeit spirit as well. Now when I talk to folk I really just want to see children injected with a degree of knowledge so they are aware of the counterfeit religions around, and the parents need to be able to teach their children."

CHRISTIAN TERMS - MORMON REDEFINITIONS

Here are some examples of major Christian doctrinal terms the meanings of which have been "amended" by Mormons. [49]

Mormonism	The Bible
Preexistence	
We all exist eternally.	Only God preexisted, (John 8:58, Col. 1.17). There is no spiritual existence prior to earth, (1 Cor. 15:46).
The Fall	
It brought mortality & physical death - not fallen nature. Adam was given two conflicting commands & was supposed to fall.	God tempts no one, (James 1:13,14) Mankind is basically sinful, (Romans 8:5-8, 1 Cor. 1:21).
Sin	
Not man's basic nature but specific acts.	We are in spiritual rebellion until conversion, (Eph. 2:3 & Romans 5:6), we don't just commit sins - we are basically sinful, (Matt. 1:21).
Repentance	
We need to repent of individual acts - not sinful nature.	We must repent of basic rebellion to God, (Jer. 17:9 & Luke 5:32).
Atonement - Salvation by grace	
Christ's death brought release from the grave & universal resurrection but one must still earn his/her own place in heaven	Salvation is not universal but is based on the belief of each individual (Romans 1:16, Hebrews 9:28, Eph. 2:8-9).
Redeemed	
Only from mortal death, not sinful rebellion or spiritual death.	Christ redeems us from spiritual death, (Romans 6:23, Eph. 2:1).
Gospel	
Mormon church system & doctrines.	The message of Jesus Christ's Death & resurrection as atonement in full for our sins, (1 Cor. 15:1-4, Gal. 1:8).
Born Again	
Being baptised into the LDS church.	We are spiritually dead until our spiritual rebirth, (John 3:3, 1 Peter 1:23, 2 Cor.5:17).

Mormonism	The Bible
True Church	
Only the LDS church - the true church was taken from earth until restored by Joseph Smith.	Born-again Christians are all part of God's church, (1 Cor. 12:12-14, Matt. 18:19-20, Matt. 16:18).
Authority - Priesthood	
Only LDS have authority to baptise, ordain etc.; two priesthoods, of Melchizedek & Aaron.	Christ ended Aaronic priesthood, & is the exclusive Priest of Melchizedek, (Heb. 5:9-10, 7:24, 2 Peter 2:9-10, & Rev. 1:6).
Baptism	
Must be performed by LDS priesthood.	Emphasis is on the believer, not the priesthood, (Mark 16:15-16).
Sons of God	
We are all literal spirit children of God.	We become a child of God at conversion, (John 1:12).
Eternal Life	
Exaltation in Celestial Kingdom - ability to bear children in heaven - must have temple marriage.	Given to all Christians eternally, with heavenly parenthood or temple marriages not mentioned, (1 John 5:12-13).
Immortality	
Universal gift - ability to live forever, but not eternal life.	No Bible distinction between immortality & eternal life, (2 Tim. 1:10).
Heaven	
Divided into 3 kingdoms, a place for everyone (misuse of 1 Cor. 15:40-41).	Only mentions two choices - everlasting punishment or eternal life with Jesus, (Matt. 25:31-46).
Kingdom of God	
Celestial kingdom only in God's presence.	All redeemed believers will be in God's presence, (Rev. 21:1-3, Matt. 13:41-43)
Hell	
An eternal institution where inmates come & go as a jail (released when debt is paid to God), but don't spend eternity there.	A place of eternal punishment from which there is no release, (Rev. 21:8, Matt. 13:24-43 & 47-50, Luke 16:26).
Godhead	
Father God is resurrected man with physical body. Christ is another resurrected man also with physical body, Holy Ghost also separate with spiritual body; result = 3	God is not a man (Numb. 23:19), there is only one God (Deut. 6:4, Is. 43:10-11, Is. 44:6, 45:21-22) Father is Spirit and invisible, (John 4:24, 1 Tim. 1:17).
Holy Ghost	
A person separate from both Father & Son; also separate from the Holy Spirit which is only an influence from the Father and not personal.	Ghost & Spirit is the same Greek word so there is no distinction; He is personal & one with the Father & the Son (1 Cor. 3:16, 6:19, 1 John 5:7)

Virgin Birth

The Father, as a resurrected physical man, had sexual relations with Mary, so Jesus was conceived the same way as all mankind.	The Holy Spirit came upon Mary & created a physical body for Jesus within her (Matt. 1:18, Hebrews 10:5)

Christians and Mormons may use the same or similar terms but you can see how the Mormon leaders have given them totally different meanings. They have little in common, and the Mormon meanings are rejected by Christians. Imagine an operating theatre where one of the nursing assistants decided to rename all the surgical instruments. The surgeon asks for a scalpel, the nurse give a saw- such a nurse would be evicted and disciplined very quickly. Spiritually that is what the Mormon Church leadership have done. They have many things to change and put right before they could be seriously considered a "Christian" church.

FACTS YOU WON'T BE TOLD WHEN MORMON MISSIONARIES CALL AT YOUR DOOR

Maybe your street has recently had another visit from the Mormon Missionaries. They were promoting the rather unorthodox religious beliefs of the Church of Jesus Christ of Latter-day Saints of Salt Lake City, Utah, USA. As a concerned neighbour you might be interested in some facts about this religious organisation. Mormons go to great lengths to appear "Christian" when they present their beliefs and their church to you. But they won't tell you the full story. *(We have found many of them don't even know the truth about their own church.)*

Mormons won't tell you that their Prophet, Joseph Smith Jnr., was heavily involved in the Occult, Spiritism and Freemasonry when he founded Mormonism.

Mormons won't tell you that they encourage visitations from dead relatives from the "spirit world," a practice repeatedly forbidden in the Bible.

Mormons won't tell you that their secret temple oaths are based on the same oaths used in Freemasonry's Blue Lodge. These are gruesome, including ripping out the tongue, the heart and the stomach if the secrets are shared with a non-Mormon.

Mormons won't tell you that they considered the Negro race and all brown-skinned people to be inferior, having the "Curse of Cain" because of their skin colour and curly hair. People of such races were forbidden entry into Mormon temples and priesthood orders until 1978.

Mormons won't tell you that Joseph Smith taught there were inhabitants of the moon who dressed like Quakers and lived to about 1,000 years of age. Brigham Young, Smith's replacement, taught there were similar inhabitants on the sun as well.

Mormons won't tell you that their prophet Joseph Smith did not die as a martyr as they claim, but was killed during a gun battle while he, his brother Hyrum & several friends were trying to escape from the Carthage jail. Smith killed two men and wounded a third. He also gave the Masonic hailing sign of distress while being gunned down. Martyrs don't shoot back!

Mormons won't tell you that they intend to become gods themselves one day, and are helping to earn their exaltation to godhood by talking to you.

Mormons won't tell you that women receive salvation only through their Mormon husbands, and must remain pregnant for all eternity.

Mormons won't tell you that they intend to have many wives in heaven, until they have enough children to populate their own planet.

Mormons won't tell you that the "heavenly father" they ask you to pray to with them is really an exalted, evolved man who lives on a planet near the imaginary starbase Kolob, and is not the Heavenly Father of the Christian Bible at all.

Mormons won't tell you that the Virgin Mary really wasn't a virgin at all, but had a normal marriage sexual relationship with their heavenly father to produce the Mormon version of Jesus.

Mormons won't tell you that they believe Jesus is really Lucifer's brother in the spirit world, and it was only due to a heavenly council of gods which voted that the Mormon Jesus should become the earth's redeemer and Saviour, instead of Lucifer/Satan.

Mormons won't tell you that they believe Jesus of Nazareth had three wives - two Mary's and Martha - plus several children while he lived on earth. Since Mormons believe that only married men get to become gods, Jesus had to be married to fit into their beliefs.

Mormons won't tell you that their so-called inspired scriptures *(The Book of Mormon, Pearl of Great Price & Doctrines & Covenants)* which no Christian group accepts, all contradict each other as well as the Bible.

Mormons won't tell you that the reason the Book of Mormon has no map because there is no evidence to support it, not even for one of the 38 major cities it claims existed. *(The holy books of every world religion have maps to prove their beginnings.)* Even the highly regarded Smithsonian Institute of Washington discredited the archeological and linguistic claims of the Book of Mormon, including the half million casualties claimed to have fallen at Cumorah, New York, in 385 AD. The Mormon Church says it has evidence to support its claims, but refuses to allow any independent testing.

Mormons won't tell you that the three witnesses *(Cowdery, Whitmer & Harris)* claimed by Joseph Smith to have seen the gold plates from which the Book of Mormon was alleged to have been translated, all left the Mormon Church and each later testified publicly none of them ever saw the gold plates. Cowdery also accused Smith of adultery *(later proven)*, lying and teaching false doctrines. Smith accused all three of being "thieves and counterfeiters." If Smith were right, why do these three still have their names printed at the beginning of every Book of Mormon, even today?

Mormons won't tell you that there have been over 4,000 changes to the Book of Mormon since it was first introduced by Smith as "The Inspired Word of God," and "The Most Perfect Book on Earth." Most of these changes were made to cover up Smith's false prophecies, including the Second Coming of Jesus Christ in 1891. 58 out of 61 of Smith's prophecies failed to happen - sure signs of a false prophet.

Mormons won't tell you that The Book of Mormon was originally written as a 'fairy-story' of what would have happened if Jesus Christ had visited America. Its real author was probably Rev. Solomon Spaulding, a Congregational minister whose Sunday school was attended by Joseph Smith Jnr. Smith obtained a copy of the manuscript, adding over 25,000 words, mainly from the Bible (especially from Isaiah, Malachi & the New Testament) and then published the book under his own name. In the original versions, Joseph Smith even claimed authorship. The granddaughter of Rev. Spaulding appeared on American television during the last decade with the original manuscript and the similarities between it and the Book of Mormon are impossible to avoid.

Mormons won't tell you that they consider the Holy Bible to be untrustworthy and full of errors. They claim parts of the Bible have been mistranslated. Mormon leaders have had over 160 years to provide evidence of this, and have yet to produce anything credible.

ɪn't tell you that they believe their church is the only right one, and churches are wrong; that all Christian creeds are an abomination; and ɜr, pastor or priest is hired by Satan to mislead you.

Mormons won't tell you that in the State of Utah, where almost 80% of the population are Mormon, there is a much higher than national average rate of divorce, wife-beating, bigamy, child abuse, teenage suicide & antidepressant use.

Conclusion: The "Church of Jesus Christ of Latter-day Saints", as Mormons call themselves, is not a Christian organisation, and it isn't based on the Bible. Mormon leaders are well aware that if these and many other facts were known to potential converts they would have very few converts. The missionaries may be well-dressed and nice young people, but many may not know the above facts or have been well trained to keep them hidden.

To The Mormon: This information has been given to you in love. We testify to you that it is accurate and honest. The people and programmes of the Mormon Church may appear good, but the best organisation and a sincere faith misdirected away from the God of the Bible will not save you. Become a seeker of the truth about the real Jesus Christ. The current President of the Mormon Church, Gordon B. Hinckley, recently admitted the Mormon Jesus Christ is not the Jesus Christ of the Bible, but a different Jesus *(see 2 Corinthians 11:4)*. Remember those missionary lessons before you joined the church? Were you asked to make an eternal decision, based on incomplete and inaccurate information? We urge you to call out to the One True God and ask Him to reveal Himself to you, and ask the One True Jesus Christ to apply His sacrifice on the cross to your sins personally.

To the Ex-Mormon: We know you were told there is no hope or help for you outside the Mormon Church. They were wrong! Tens of thousands have left and received help. Some are now available to help you, along with others who have studied this and similar cults. Please don't give up on the real God because of the errors of the Mormon Church. We especially recommend that you renounce the false baptism you may have had because of the spiritual ties and bondages this brings on members. If you have never requested that your name be removed from membership, we urge you to so in writing. Leaving your name on their list directly aids their missionary efforts. If you need spiritual help, please write to us in confidence.

To Christians & others who care: If you have a burden to reach Mormons and inform the public about the real doctrines of Mormonism, we need your help. We have materials to share. All donations are used without personal gain. People deserve to have complete and accurate information before making decisions that will determine their eternal destiny!

Tragically many Mormons are not fully aware of the doctrines and history of their own church. The Mormon Church claims to have the truth, so it must be open to honest investigation. It does not show up in a good light. If something is true it can stand being questioned. If it is not true it needs to be questioned!

(The above information reflects current teaching of the Mormon Church at time of printing)

THREE POSSIBILITIES - "WILL YOU GAMBLE WITH YOUR ETERNAL LIFE?

Possibility 1. It is possible both Mormonism & the Christian Church, while sincere, are wrong about the Truth. Both would then be false religions

Possibility 2. It is possible Mormonism is right about the Truth, & the Christian Church is wrong. If this is true, that Mormonism as brought forth by Joseph Smith Jnr is God's restored Gospel; then the Christian Church is wrong & is an apostate faith.

Possibility 3. It is possible the Christian Church is right about the Truth, & that Mormonism is wrong. This would mean that the historic Christian faith is the true Gospel; & that Mormonism is an apostate faith.

What are the implications of these three choices?

1. If the first option is correct, then both Mormonism & the Christians are wrong. Perhaps Hinduism Islam or Jehovah's Witnesses are correct, or even the Atheist! We need to explore all avenues to Truth.

2. If Mormonism is correct, then the Mormon is right and the Christian is wrong. Mormons inherit the Celestial Kingdom. Mormon Apostle Bruce McConkie agreed that Christians would attain the Terrestrial Kingdom. (M D page 784). Jesus is evident there, according to D & C 76:77. Not a bad place to end up!

3. If the Christian is right & the Mormon is wrong, and there is a heaven and a hell, nothing good is in store for anyone losing this choice. Only true followers of Jesus Christ will be permitted to spend eternity with Him. (Hebrews 12:23; John 3:16-21; Rev. 2:11; 20:6)

Hell is for unbelievers. (Matt. 8:12; 25:41-46). It is eternal separation from God in a painful, final and everlasting state (Rev 14:10-11; 2 Thess. 1:9)

HOW TO PRAY EFFECTIVELY FOR LATTER-DAY SAINTS

* The first matter to understand is that the battle is spiritual. Ephesians 6:12 says **"For we do not wrestle against flesh and blood** (your relative/friend) **but against principalities, against powers, against the rulers of darkness of this age, against spiritual hosts of wickedness in heavenly places."** We are not fighting your loved one. They are in spiritual bondage. We are going to deal with the demonic spirits which blind and deafen them to the true Gospel of Jesus Christ, and which prevent them responding to Him.

* Make sure there is no unconfessed sin in your life. If so, get it right with God. Then know your authority in Christ to overcome all the power of the evil ones. **"I give you the authority to trample on serpents and scorpions** (demons)**, and over all the power of the enemy, and nothing shall by any means hurt you. Nevertheless, do not rejoice in this, that the spirits are subject to you, but rather rejoice because your names are written in heaven,"** (Luke 10:19-20).

* If possible, ask another Christian believer to agree with you in prayer. **"...If two of you agree on earth concerning anything you ask, it will be done for you by My Father in heaven,"** (Matthew 18:19). What if you are alone, and have no-one to agree with you? Lori MacGregor (a former cult member who now heads up a Christian ministry to reach people in cults) recommends you ask Jesus or the Holy Spirit to agree with you. Then pray to God in the name of the Saviour Jesus Christ as the Holy Spirit directs you.

* Bind the principal demonic strongman, "The Spirit of Moroni," in the name of Jesus Christ. **"Assuredly, I say to you, whatever you bind on earth will be bound in heaven..,"** (Matthew 18:18). Other demonic spirits which need to be bound include; Antichrist, Unbelief, Error, False Doctrine, Confusion, Legalism, Guilt, Fear of Church Authorities, etc. (ask the Holy Spirit for the names or effects caused by these and other demonic spirits, and how to remove their influence from your loved one.)

* Ask God to release and loose your relative/friend from these demonic spirits and all others which control them. **"...Whatever you loose on earth will be loosed in heaven,"** (Matthew 18:18).

* Ask the Lord to release your loved one's emotions, which have been held in fear and bondage for so long. The Holy Spirit will do this gently and lovingly, so that

the person comes to understand who they really are, and how much Jesus really loves them.

* Be assured that God is now at work in their lives to release them from their bondage. Pray for their salvation, in faith. If the person is a family member, God's promise to you is to **"Believe on the Lord Jesus Christ, and you shall be saved, you and your household,"** (Acts 16:31). If they are not a family member, God gives another promise for you to appropriate in prayer for them. **"The Lord is not slack concerning His promise... but is longsuffering towards us, not willing that any should perish but that all should come to repentance,"** (2 Peter 3:9) and **"God our Saviour... desires all men to be saved and to come to the knowledge of the truth,"** (1 Timothy, 2:4). God's Word is plain, He doesn't want your relative/friend in the Latter-day Saints to perish, to be wiped out on Judgement Day. God wants them saved, and we have a commission from Him to do the job in prayer, and to find out how.

* Keep on praying in faith for your loved one. Experience shows that perseverance produces the best results, so don't be discouraged if there are no positive signs for a while. Ask the Lord to make His word alive to them, to show them the truth, even from their Scriptures.

PRAYER OF RENUNCIATION & RELEASE

for those previously involved in the Church of Jesus Christ of the Latter-day Saints.

If you have ever held Bible studies with Mormon missionaries, or attended one of their church buildings or temples, or been baptised by the Latter-day Saints Church, etc., then you will need to repent of these involvements before God, ask His forgiveness, plead guilty without excuse, then **"...Confess with your mouth** (out loud) **that Jesus is Lord, and believe in your heart that God raised Him from the dead,"** (Romans 10:9). Then ask Jesus to come in and be Lord of your life. Ask the Holy Spirit to come and fill you, removing all traces of the deceptions of the Latter-day Saints, to help you understand the Bible the way God wrote it, and to help you build up your relationship with Jesus every day. To help you with these matters may we suggest the following prayer.

(Please pause briefly following each paragraph to allow the Holy Spirit to show any additional issues which He may wish to bring to your attention)

"Father God, creator of the heavens and the earth, I come to you in the name of Jesus Christ your Son. I come as a sinner seeking forgiveness and cleansing from all sins I have committed against you, and against all others made in your image.

I honour my earthly father and mother, and all of my ancestors of flesh and blood, and of the spirit by adoption, but I utterly turn away from and renounce all their sins. I forgive all in my family line for the effects of their sins on me and my children. I confess and renounce all of my own sins. I renounce and rebuke Satan and every power of his affecting me and my family.

In the name of Jesus Christ, I renounce every action and word of mine which gave others permission to deceive and control me. I renounce, forsake and break every covenant I have ever made with the Church of Jesus Christ of the Latter-day Saints. I renounce and forsake the false headship and authority of the President and the General Authorities, all Quoram of the Twelve Apostles; all members of the Presidency of the Seventy; all members of the Second Quoram of the Seventy; and all Presiding Bishoprics; and their idolatrous usurping of their organisation in the place of the Lord Jesus Christ.

In the name of Jesus Christ, I renounce and forsake the heretical writings of Joseph Smith Jnr; Brigham Young; all Presidents, all General Authorities, and all other writings published by the Church of Jesus Christ of Latter-day Saints. Lord Jesus, help me to honour you by removing all these books and publications from my home and life, and I cut off every bondage I have been under because of those writings, in the name of Jesus Christ.

In the name of Jesus Christ I renounce and cut off my life the ungodly Covenants of Baptism and Membership of the Church of Jesus Christ of Latter-day Saints; including all false Aaronic and Melchizedek Priesthoods, and all the witchcraft and Masonic oaths invoked in those initiation ceremonies. I renounce these and all other ungodly soul ties, and I command the spirits which empower those soul ties to leave me now in the name of Jesus Christ. I gather those soul ties together and sever them through with the Sword of the Spirit of God, and humbly request the blood of Jesus Christ to seal those ends so they will never be able to reconnect.

Lord Jesus, you are the wonderful Counsellor, and you know all my problems, all those things which bind, torment, defile and harass me. I now confess that my body is the temple of the Holy Spirit, redeemed, cleansed and sanctified by the blood of Jesus Christ.

I ask you, Lord Jesus, to fill me now with your Holy Spirit, so that He will give me insight and understanding when I read and study your Word. I enthrone you, Lord Jesus in my heart, for you are my Lord and Saviour, the source of eternal life. Thank you, Father God, for your mercy, your forgiveness and your love, in the name of Jesus Christ. Amen."

It is very important that you write to your national Mormon Church and sever your ties with them. If you were a member and/or baptised by them, you will need to formally resign and request your name be removed from ALL their lists, including those in Salt Lake City, Utah, and elsewhere. Ask for written confirmation that this has been done. It is known there are several thousand names on their New Zealand membership register belonging to people who have ceased supporting the LDS Church but who have neglected to have their names removed. Spiritual ties can continue for many until their names have been removed from the register, in conjunction with the prayer recommended above. Both actions are essential.

WHERE DO I TURN?

If you have difficulty going through this prayer, then please contact any of those listed below. (Jubilee has links with ministries which can assist in most countries world-wide); or contact a competent Christian leader near you to assist you. Find Bible-believing Christians and spend time with them. Please explain to them you are coming out of a deceptive cult and need their encouragement and support at least until you are firmly on your feet. If some disappoint you (probably through not understanding your need) don't be put off, for there are caring Christians around who can and will help.

Jubilee Resources, PO Box 36-044, Wellington 6330, New Zealand,
Jubilee Resources, PO Box 1412, Sunnybank Hills, Qld 4109, Australia,
Jubilee Resources, PO Box 4174, Evansville IN 47724-4174, USA,
Jubilee Resources, PO New Hamburg, Ontario N0B 2G0 Canada
Mount Carmel Outreach, PO Box 491, Carmel, IN 46032, USA
Saints Alive, PO Box 1076, Issaquah, WA 98027, USA
Utah Lighthouse Ministry, P.O. Box 1884, Salt Lake City, Utah 84110, USA.
MacGregor Ministries, Box 294, Nelson, B.C., V1L 5P9, Canada

REFERENCES

1. Journal of Discourses, vol. 16, p. 46
2. Doctrines of Salvation, vol. 1, p. 188
3. Joseph Smith History, 1:19; The Seer, Apostle Orson Pratt, p. 255 & 212; & Pearl of Great Price, J. Smith 2:19
3a Heresies Exposed, W C Irvine, p. 127
4. Discourses of Brigham Young, p. 116; & Journal of Discourses vol. 7, p. 289
5. Mormon Doctrine, p. 169
6. Christian Deviations, p. 112
7. Mormonism Unveiled p. 261; Heresies Exposed, p. 121
8. Mormon Claims Answered, by Marvin Cowan, p. 9
9. Heresies Exposed, p. 121-2
10. History of the Church, vol. 4, p. 551-2; vol. 5, p. 2
11. History of the Church, vol. 2, p. 18
11a Joseph Smith's Teaching, by E.F. Parry, p. 86
12. Mormons are a Peculiar People, pps. 110-167
13. Kingdom of the Cults, p. 175
14. History of the Church, vol. 7, p. 102-3; Vol. 6, pps. 617-618; The Gospel Kingdom by John Taylor p. 360
15. Christian Deviations, p. 115
16. To Moroni with Love, by Ed Decker p. 30
17. History of the Church, vol. 4, p. 461
18. Mormon Claims Answered, p. 40
19. Christian Deviations, p. 119
20. Kingdom of the Cults, pps. 184-5
21. Read chapters 8 & 9 of *"Reasoning from the Scriptures with the Mormons," by Ron Rhodes,for one of the best examples of proving the inerrancy and authority of the Bible.*
22. Gleanings by the Way, J.A. Clark, p. 256
23. Palmyra Reflector, March 19, 1831
24. Mormon Claims Answered, p. 56
24a Times and Seasons, p. 482 & elsewhere
25. A Book of Mormon Study, by Brigham Roberts, pt. 2,4, p. 17
25a The Book of Mormon Difficulties, by Brigham Roberts
26. The True Origin of the B.O.M., Shook, pps. 94 & 126; Mormonism Unveiled, E.D. Howe, p. 278
27. The Four Major Cults, p. 30
28. Is Mormonism Christian? p. 10
29. The Maze of Mormonism, p. 45
30. The Seer, p. 255
31. A Summary Critique - Are Mormons Christians? by Gordon R. Lewis, CRJournal, Fall, 1992, p 33
32. The Utah Christians Tract Society newsletter March/April 1978
33. History of the Church, vol. 6, p 305
34. The Gospel through the Ages, pps. 105-6
35. Doctrines & Covenants, 130:22
36. Pearl of Great Price, p. 60
37. Journal of Discourses, vol. 1, p. 50
38. Adapted from Cultwatch, pps. 20-1
39. A Marvellous Work and a Wonder, pps. 67-8
40. Pearl of Great Price, Joseph Smith History 1:68-73
41. Book of Abraham 1:21,22,27
42. Doctrines & Salvation 3:247
43. Book of Mormon, Alma 10:3
44. Kingdom of the Cults, p. 198
45. Prophet John Taylor, in Journal of Discourses, vol 6:163
46. LDS Temple Ceremony of Garden of Eden, quoted in What's Going on in There? p. 28
47. Mormon Doctrine, by Bruce R. McConkie, 1958 edition, p 477
48. 1 Nephi 12:23; 2 Nephi 5:21; Journal of Discourses, vol. 7, p. 290; Mormon Doctrine, pps. 526-7
49. adapted from a leaflet by Jerald and Sandra Tanner (former Mormons)
50. The Evangel, published by The Utah Missions, Inc., vol. xli no. 4, May 1994, p. 1
51. Mormon Claims Answered, p. 57
53. Doctrines & Covenants, 84:2-5, 31
55.Gospel through the Ages, by Milton R. Hunter, pps. 15, 93-99; Journal of Discourse, vol. xi, p., 122
56. History of the Church, vol. 6, pps. 308, 474

RECOMMENDED READING AND VIEWING

"Kingdom of the Cults," by Dr. Walter Martin, (Bethany House Publishers)
"Cult Watch" by John Ankerberg & Dr. John Weldon, (Harvest House)
"Mormon Claims Answered," by Marvin W. Cowan
"To Moroni With Love," by Ed Decker, (Huntington House)
"Reasoning from the Scriptures with the Mormons," by Ron Rhodes, (Harvest House)
"Mormonism," by Kurt Van Gordon, (Zondervan)
"The Mormon Mirage," Latayne Colvett Scott, (Zondervan)
"Beyond Mormonism - an Elder's Story," By James Spencer, (Chosen Books)
"Changing World of Mormonism," Jerald & Sandra Tanner, (Moody)
"Larson's Book of Cults," by Bob Larson, (Tyndale)
"So What's the Difference," by Fritz Ridenour, (Regal Books)
"Heresies Exposed," by Wm. C. Irvine, (Scripture Literature Press)
"Christian Deviations- the Challenge of the Sects," by Horton Davies, (SCM Press)
"What's Going on in there?" by Chuck Sackett
Video; "The Mormon Dilemma" by Jeremiah Films, available from most Christian video libraries.

STOP PRESS

As I completed the manuscript for this book, I received the following press clipping from the United States. "STERLING, VA. Michael J. Barrett, who is assistant general council for the Central Intelligence Agency and a long-time member of the LDS church has been excommunicated from the Mormon Church. Barrett's Stake President, F. LeMar Sleight has stated that Barrett was excommunicated for disobedience because the ***"public has no business knowing about church history and doctrine."***

Mr. Barrett has been rather outspoken on LDS church history and doctrine and the changes and cover-ups the church has perpetrated in the past. (His letters had previously appeared in many of the leading newspapers throughout the United States and Britain.) Barrett also relates that on two separate occasions F. Burton Howard and F. Enzio Busche, members of the First Quorum of the Seventy (a senior level of church leaders) have told him **that the LDS church has an obligation to conceal its doctrines; that we are trying to become a mainstream Christian church"** Barrett's response was, *"I'm in a Catch-22: If I tell the truth about our doctrines and history I get excommunicated. If I lie about the gospel, then Christ will condemn me for conceit about the Gospel."*[50]

Is the quest for truth and honesty too dangerous for Mormon leaders? Barrett is absolutely right - We all have to answer to Jesus, one day soon!

SUMMARY

I have had to simplify quite complex issues into just a few lines in this book, but many have confirmed that I have succeeded in presenting a balanced look at both the Mormon beliefs and practices, and compared them with the Biblical Christian view. We have seen some of the many contradictions which the Mormon Tenth Prophet said we would find if Mormonism were a fraud. We have looked briefly at the occultic activities of the founder. We have seen the Book of Mormon fail the tests of divine inspiration as well as factual evidence. We have also seen how the Book of Mormon doesn't even teach most major Mormon doctrines, and in fact contradicts it. We have read how the three witnesses witnessed only a fraud.

Mormon men have been short-changed, for they do not qualify for the true Aaronic and Melchizedek priesthoods because the first was cancelled, and the second belongs exclusively to Jesus Christ. Mormon men are not gods in embryo. Mormon priestly authority and baptism is actually invalid. Mormonism falls far short of the New Testament Priesthood of all Believers. Mormonism fails the every Bible test, proving it still isn't Christian. Merely claiming the title "Christian" doesn't make it true. The doctrines and practices must be aligned with the Bible. Jesus Christ did away with temple worship, the law and works for salvation. The Mormon Church have adopted it all back again, so their disobedience to God is rebellion. Because the Mormon Church teaches that the Bible has been intentionally mistranslated, Mormons live in a fools' paradise believing their only hope lies in their church. They fail to see that they are sinners in desperate need of the true Saviour. Any Mormon who doesn't see themselves as a sinner, doesn't see what God sees - that all men are sinners (Romans 3:23 & 2 Nephi 28:31).

We are each called to be a new creation in Christ. Those who choose the Jesus of the Bible have already been redeemed and can be certain of their salvation and eternal life, (1 John 5:13; John 17:3; John 3:36). Those who put their hope in Joseph Smith cannot have that assurance. Mormonism stands or falls on Joseph Smith, not on Jesus Christ. 1 Timothy 2:5 states that Jesus is our only mediator. But those who trust in Joseph Smith are accursed by God, according to Jeremiah 17:5. God warns us in His Word that if someone tries to tell us something inconsistent with the Bible, then it is not of God and should be rejected. **"But even if we, or an angel from heaven, preach any other gospel to you than what we have preached to you, let him be accursed,"** (Galatians 1:8). The word used here is "anathema" which is a very strong term of judgement involving being cursed by God Himself.

Joseph Smith and Brigham Young are dead. The Church of Jesus Christ of Latter -day Saints will one day disappear, and each one of us will be left to face Jesus

Christ, alone. There won't be an apostle or a bishop to plead our case. There won't be anyone from the Mormon General Authorities. They will have to face Jesus alone too. Jesus states plainly that His words will judge us on the last day. He means what He taught in the Bible, not the words of some latter day "prophet" who falsely added to God's Word. Readers are invited to test what I have written by the true Word of God - the Bible. No-one can talk with God when they have turned away from His Word. If you have genuine doubts and questions, then ask God about the authority of His Word above all else, for God honours His Word.

Is it worth your soul to be deceived? If you are in the Mormon Church, then the true Jesus Christ is calling you to come out of it, for Mormonism follows a **"different Jesus,"** it is led (and deceived) by a **"different spirit,"** and it believes a **"different Gospel."** Because these bring judgement on all who participate in such things, Jesus Christ is offering you a way out to liberty and into His Kingdom. We don't need the "One True Church" - we each need the "One True Lord Jesus." If you need prayer and support, please contact one of the ministries listed on page 45. It is the love of Jesus which compels them to offer to help you. What is your response to the True Lord Jesus Christ? He awaits you now!

Books you can order by Selwyn Stevens - *(photocopies of this order form welcome)*

Title	Code #	NZ$	US$	Aus/Can$
Unmasking Freemasonry	BFMS	$9-95	$6-00	$9-95
Unmasking Mormonism	BUMS	$9-95	$6-00	$9-95
Unmasking the Watchtower	BUWS	$9-95	$6-00	$9-95
Unmasking Spiritualism	BUSS	$9-95	$6-00	$9-95
Fatal Faith	BFFS	$9-95	$6-00	$9-95
The New Age - Old Lie in a new pack	BNAS	$9-95	$6-00	$9-95
Signs & Symbols & what they mean	BSSS	$6-95	$4-00	$6-95
Treated or Tricked - Altern. Therapies	BTTB	$12-50	$7-00	$11.95
Servant of 2 Masters - Christ. Masons	BSTS	$5-95	$3-50	$5-95
Essentials for Faith	BEFS	$9-95	$6-00	$9-95
Every Eye Shall See! - Christ's Return	BEYS	$10-95	$6-50	$10-95
How to Recognise the Voice of God	BHRS	$4-95	$3-00	$4-95
Rediscovering the Messiah in the Passover	BRMS	$4-95	$3-00	$4-95

sub-total $_______

Post & Handling$_______

Signature ________________________

(required for card payments only)

Gift for ministry$_______

TOTAL ENCLOSED $_______

Visa/Mastercard No_______/_______/_______/_______Expiry____/____

Name *(Please print)*____________________________

Address____________________________

City____________________State & Postcode__________

Country____________________________

Please post me ...... copies of latest catalogue for my friends.

ORDER FROM: Jubilee Resources

PO Box 36-044, Wellington 6330, New Zealand
PO Box 1412, Sunnybank Hills, QLD 4109, Australia
PO Box 4174, Evansville IN 47724-4174, USA
PO New Hamburg, Ontario N0B 2G0 Canada
Internet: www.jubilee-resources.com

Special note for placing orders

Most deliveries in N.Z. & Australia may be more suitable by Courier (allow 1-5 days) so please advise street address. Items dispatched to other countries sent by International Air Mail Post - please allow to 5-14 days for delivery. Visa & Mastercard payments will be transacted in the nearest currency at the rate closest to the amounts shown. NZ, Australian & Canadian prices include gst. E. & O.E.

POST & HANDLING RATES

Orders from:

New Zealand - in NZ currency
add 10% (minimum $2-50)

USA - in US currency
add 20% (minimum $3-00)

Australia - in Aust. currency
add 15% (minimum $3-00)

Canada - in Canadian currency
add 20% (minimum $4-00)

Rest of World - in US currency
add 20% (minimum $5-00)